AF148544

THE
13 STEPS TO
RICHES

Featuring Erik Swanson & Marie Diamond

ORGANIZED PLANNING
VOLUME 6

HABITUDE
WARRIOR

Foreword by Olympian Ruben Gonzalez

#1 BESTSELLER

Copyright © 2022

THE 13 STEPS TO RICHES

All rights reserved. No part of this publication may be reproduced, distributed, or transmitted in any form or by any means, including photocopying, recording, or other electronic or mechanical methods, without the prior written permission of the publisher and Habitude Warrior Int., except in the case of brief quotations embodied in critical reviews and certain other noncommercial uses permitted by copyright law. For permission requests, write to the publisher, addressed "Attention: Permissions Coordinator," at info@beyondpublishing.net

Permission was granted and approved to use Celebrity Author's testimonials and contributing chapters, quotes and thoughts throughout the book series, but it is understood that this series was not created by or published by the Napoleon Hill Foundation. Quantity sales special discounts are available on quantity purchases by corporations, associations, and others. For details, contact the publisher at the address above.

Orders by U.S. trade bookstores and wholesalers.
Email info@BeyondPublishing.net

Manufactured and printed in the United States of America and distributed globally by Beyond Publishing.

BEYOND
PUBLISHING

Library of Congress Control Number: 2022909469

ISBN Paperback: 978-1-637923-21-4

ISBN Hardcover: 978-1-63792-328-3

TESTIMONIALS
THE 13 STEPS TO RICHES

"What an honor to collaborate with so many personal development leaders from around the world as we Co-Author together honoring the amazing principles by Napoleon Hill in this new book series, *The 13 Steps to Riches*, by Habitude Warrior and Erik "Mr. Awesome" Swanson. Well done "Mr. Awesome" for putting together such an amazing series. If you want to up-level your life, read every book in this series and learn to apply each of these time tested steps and principles."

Denis Waitley ~ Author of *Psychology of Winning & The NEW Psychology of Winning - Top Qualities of a 21st Century Winner*

"Just as *Think and Grow Rich* reveals the 13 steps to success discovered by Napoleon Hill after interviewing the richest people around the world (and many who considered themselves failures) in the early 1900's, *The 13 Steps to Riches*, produced by Habitude Warrior and Erik Swanson takes a modern look at those same 13 steps. It brings together many of today's personal development leaders to share their stories of how *the 13 Steps to Riches* have created and propelled their own successes. I am honored to participate and share the power of Faith in my life. If you truly want to accelerate reaching the success you deserve, read every volume of *The 13 Steps to Riches*."

Sharon Lechter ~ 5 Time N.Y. Times Best-Selling Author. Author of *Think and Grow Rich for Women*, Co-Author of *Exit Rich*, *Rich Dad Poor Dad*, *Three Feet from Gold*, *Outwitting the Devil* and *Success and Something Greater* ~ **SharonLechter.com**

"The most successful book on personal achievement ever written is now being elaborated upon by many of the world's top thought leaders. I'm honored to Co-Author this series on the amazing principles from Napoleon Hill, in *The 13 Steps to Riches*, by Habitude Warrior, Erik "Mr. Awesome" Swanson."

> *Jim Cathcart* ~ Best-Selling Author of *Relationship Selling* and *The Acorn Principle,* among many others. Certified Speaking Professional (CSP) and Former President of the National Speakers Association (NSA)

"Some books are written to be read and placed on the shelf. Others are written to transform the reader, as they travel down a path of true transcendence and enlightenment. "*The 13 steps to Riches*" by Habitude Warrior and Erik Swanson is the latter. Profoundly insightful, it revitalizes the techniques and strategies written by Napoleon Hill by applying a modern perspective, and a fearsome collaboration of some of the greatest minds and thought leaders from around the globe. A must read for all of those who seek to break free of their current levels of success, and truly extract the greatness that lies within. It is an honor and a privilege to have been selected to participate, in what is destined to be the next historic chapter in the meteoric rise of many men and women around the world."

> *Glenn Lundy* ~ Husband to one, Father to 8, Automotive Industry Expert, Author of "The Morning 5", Creator of the popular morning show "#riseandgrind", and the Founder of "Breakfast With Champions"

"How exciting to team up with the amazing Habitude Warrior community of leaders such as Erik Swanson, Sharon Lechter, John Assaraf, Denis Waitley and so many more transformational and self-help icons to bring you these timeless and proven concepts in the fields of success and wealth. *The 13 Steps to Riches* book series will help you reach your dreams and accomplish your goals faster than you have ever experienced before!"

> *Marie Diamond* ~ Featured in *The Secret*, Modern Day Spiritual Teacher, Inspirational Speaker, Feng Shui Master

"If you are looking to crystalize your mightiest dream, rekindle your passion, breakthrough limiting beliefs and learn from those who have done exactly what you want to do - read this book! In this transformational masterpiece, *The 13 Steps to Riches*, self-development guru Erik Swanson has collected the sage wisdom and time tested truths from subject matter experts and amalgamated it into a one-stop-shop resource library that will change your life forever!"

> *Dan Clark* ~ Speaker Hall of Fame & N.Y. Times Best-Selling Author of *The Art of Significance*

"Life has always been about who you surround yourself with. I am in excellent company with this collaboration from my fellow authors and friends, paying tribute to the life changing principles by Napoleon Hill in this amazing new book series, *The 13 Steps to Riches*, organized by Habitude Warrior's founder and my dear friend, Erik Swanson. Hill said, 'Your big opportunity may be right where you are now.' This book series is a must-read for anyone who wants to change their life and prosper, starting now."

> *Alec Stern* ~ America's Startup Success Expert, Co-Founder of Constant Contact

"Finally a book series that encompasses the lessons the world needs to learn and apply, but in our modern day era. As I always teach my students to "Say **YES**, and then figure out how", I strongly urge you to do the same. Say YES to adding all of these 13 books in *The 13 Steps to Riches* book series into your success library and watch both your business as well as your personal life grow as a result."

> *Loral Langemeier* ~ 5 Time N.Y. Times Best-Selling Author, Featured in *The Secret*, Author of *The Millionaire Maker* and *YES! Energy - The Equation to Do Less, Make More*

"Napoleon Hill had a tremendous impact on my consciousness when I was very young – there were very few books nor the type of trainings that we see today to lead us to success. Whenever you have the opportunity to read and harness *The 13 Steps to Riches* as they are presented in this series, be happy (and thankful) that there were many of us out there applying the principles, testing the teachings, making the mistakes, and now being offered to you in a way that they are clear, simple and concise – with samples and distinctions that will make it easier for you to design a successful life which includes adding value to others, solving world problems, and making the world work for 100% of humanity… Read on… those dreams are about to come true!"

Doria Cordova ~ CEO of Money & You, Excellerated Business School, Global Business Developer, Ambassador of New Education

"Success leaves clues and the Co-Authors in this awesome book series, *The 13 Steps to Riches*, will continue the Napoleon Hill legacy with tools, tips and modern-day principals that greatly expand on the original masterpiece… *Think and Grow Rich*. If you are serious about living your life to the max, get this book series now!"

John Assaraf ~ Chairman & CEO NeuroGym, MrNeuroGym.com, New York Times best-selling author of *Having It All, Innercise*, and *The Answer*. Also featured in *The Secret*

"Over the years, I have been blessed with many rare and amazing opportunities to invest my time and energy. These opportunities require a keen eye and immediate action. This is one of those amazing opportunities for you as a reader! I highly recommend you pick up every book in this series of *The 13 Steps to Riches* by Habitude Warrior and Erik Swanson! Learn from modern day leaders who have embraced the lessons from the great Napoleon Hill in his classic book from 1937, *Think and Grow Rich*."

Kevin Harrington ~ Original "Shark" on *Shark Tank*, Creator of the Infomercial, Pioneer of the *As Seen on TV* brand, Co-Author of *Mentor to Millions*

"When you begin your journey, you will quickly learn of the importance of the first step of *The 13 Steps To Riches*. A burning desire is the start of all worthwhile achievements. Erik 'Mr. Awesome' Swanson's newest book series contains a wealth of assistance to make your journey both successful and enjoyable. Start today... because tomorrow is not guaranteed on your calendar."

Don Green ~ 45 Years of Banking, Finance & Entrepreneurship, Best-Selling Author of *Everything I know About Success I Learned From Napoleon Hill* & *Napoleon Hill My Mentor: Timeless Principles to Take Your Success to the Next Level* & *Your Millionaire Mindset*

Our minds become magnetized with the dominating thoughts we hold in our minds and these magnets attract to us the forces, the people, the circumstances of life which harmonize with the nature of our dominating thoughts.

(Napoleon Hill)

Global Speakers Mastermind & Habitude Warrior Masterminds

Join us and become a member of our tribe! Our Global Speakers Mastermind is a virtual group of amazing thinkers and leaders who meet twice a month. Sessions are designed to be 'to the point' and focused, while sharing fantastic techniques to grown your mindset as well as your pocket books. We also include famous guest speaker spots for our private Masterclasses. We also designate certain sessions for our members to mastermind with each other & counsel on the topics discussed in our previous Masterclasses. It's time for you to join a tribe who truly cares about **YOU** and your future and start surrounding yourself with the famous leaders and mentors of our time. It is time for you to up-level your life, businesses, and relationships.

For more information to check out our Masterminds:
Team@HabitudeWarrior.com
www.DecideTobeAwesome.com

FREE GIFT!
GRAB YOUR SPECIAL
& AWESOME FREE GIFT!

We have a very special gift for those who want to surround themselves with a tribe of people creating magic in supporting each other and their growth in their personal and professional lives! It's time for you to be up-leveled in such a fantastic way! You deserve to reward yourself and join us. "NDSO!" No Drama - Serve Others!

Visit the QR code link above to get your FREE GIFT!
www.RideAlongGuestPass.com

NAPOLEON HILL

I would like to personally acknowledge and thank the one and only Napoleon Hill for his work, dedication, and most importantly believing in himself. His unwavering belief in himself, whether he realized this or not, had been passed down from generation to generation to millions and millions of individuals across this planet including me!

I'm sure, at first, as many of us experience throughout our lives as well, he most likely had his doubts. Think about it. Being offered to work for Andrew Carnegie for a full 20 years with zero pay and no guarantee of success had to be a daunting decision. But, I thank you for making that decision years and years ago. It paved the path for countless many who have trusted in themselves and found success in their own rights. You gave us all hope and desire to bank on the most important entity in our world today - ourselves!

For this, I thank you Sir, from the bottom of my heart and the top of all of our bank accounts. Let us all follow the 13 Steps to Riches and prosper in so many areas of our lives.

~ Erik "Mr Awesome" Swanson
13 Time #1 Best-Selling Author & Student of Napoleon Hill Philosophies

CPL. HUMBERTO A. SANCHEZ, 22

It is our distinct honor to dedicate each one of our *13 Steps to Riches* book volumes to each of the 13 United States Service Members who courageously lost their lives in Kabul in August, 2021. Your honor, dignity, and strength will always be cherished and remembered. ~ Habitude Warrior Team

Cpl. Humberto A. Sanchez, 22, of Logansport, Indiana, a rifleman.

His awards and decorations include the Marine Corps Good Conduct Medal, National Defense Service Medal, Sea Service Deployment Ribbon, Global War on Terrorism Service Medal. Additional awards pending approval may include Purple Heart, Combat Action Ribbon and Sea Service Deployment Ribbon. We honor you and thank you for your ultimate sacrifice!

THE 13 STEPS TO RICHES FEATURING:

DENIS WAITLEY ~ Author of *Psychology of Winning & The NEW Psychology of Winning - Top Qualities of a 21st Century Winner,* NASA's Performance Coach, Featured in *The Secret* ~ www.DenisWaitley.com

SHARON LECHTER ~ 5 Time N.Y. Times Best-Selling Author. Author of *Think and Grow Rich for Women,* Co-Author of *Exit Rich, Rich Dad Poor Dad, Three Feet from Gold, Outwitting the Devil* and *Success and Something Greater* ~ www.SharonLechter.com

JIM CATHCART~ Best-Selling Author of *Relationship Selling* and *The Acorn Principle,* among many others. Certified Speaking Professional (CSP) and Former President of the National Speakers Association (NSA) ~ www.Cathcart.com

MICHAEL E. GERBER ~ New York Times Bestseller of the mega best selling theory for over two consecutive decades… E-Myth books.

GLENN LUNDY ~ Husband to one, Father to 8, Automotive Industry Expert, Author of "The Morning 5", Creator of the popular morning show "#riseandgrind", and the Founder of "Breakfast With Champions" ~ www.GlennLundy.com

MARIE DIAMOND ~ Featured in *The Secret*, Modern Day Spiritual Teacher, Inspirational Speaker, Feng Shui Master ~ www.MarieDiamond.com

DAN CLARK ~ Award Winning Speaker, Speaker Hall of Fame, N.Y. Times Best-Selling Author of *The Art of Significance* ~ www.DanClark.com

ALEC STERN ~ America's Startup Success Expert, Co-Founder of Constant Contact, Speaker, Mentor, Investor ~ www.AlecSpeaks.com

ERIK SWANSON ~ 13 Time #1 International Best-Selling Author, Award Winning Speaker, Featured on Tedx Talks and Amazon Prime TV. Founder & CEO of the Habitude Warrior Brand ~ www.SpeakerErikSwanson.com

LORAL LANGEMEIER ~ 5 Time N.Y. Times Best-Selling Author, Featured in *The Secret*, Author of *The Millionaire Maker* and *YES! Energy - The Equation to Do Less, Make More* ~ www.LoralLangemeier.com

DORIA CORDOVA ~ CEO of Money & You, Excellerated Business School, Global Business Developer, Ambassador of New Education ~ www.FridaysWithDoria.com

JOHN ASSARAF ~ Chairman & CEO NeuroGym, MrNeuroGym.com, N. Y. Times best-selling author of *Having It All, Innercise,* and *The Answer.* Also featured in *The Secret* ~ www.JohnAssaraf.com

KEVIN HARRINGTON ~ Original "Shark" on the hit TV show *Shark Tank,* Creator of the Infomercial, Pioneer of the *As Seen on TV* brand, Co-Author of *Mentor to Millions* ~ www.KevinHarrington.TV

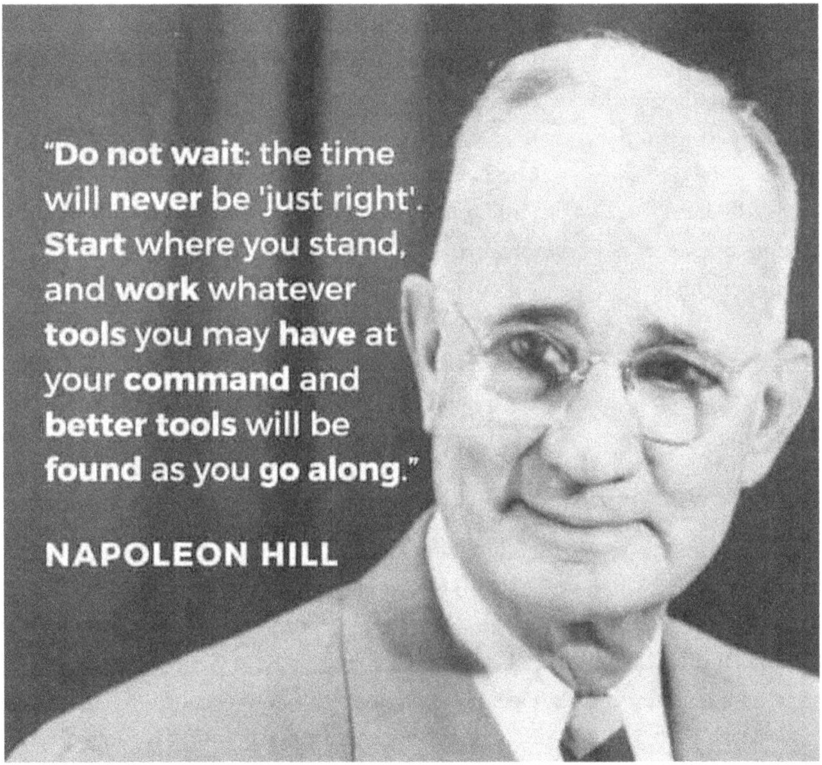

"**Do not wait**: the time will **never** be 'just right'. **Start** where you stand, and **work** whatever **tools** you may **have** at your **command** and **better tools** will be **found** as you **go along**."

NAPOLEON HILL

CONTENTS

INTRODUCTION

by Don Green

ERIK SWANSON & DON GREEN

Once you give yourself the gift of reading Erik Swanson's newest book series, *The 13 Steps to Riches*, you are sure to realize why he has earned his nickname, *"Mr. Awesome."* Readers usually read books for two reasons – they want to be entertained or they want to improve their knowledge in a certain subject. Mr. Awesome's new book series will help you do both.

I urge you to not only read this great book series in its entirety, but also apply the principles held within into your our life. Use the experience Erik Swanson has gained to reach your own level of success. I highly encourage you to invest in yourself by reading self-help materials, such as *The 13 Steps to Riches*, and I truly know you will discover that it will be one of the best investments you could ever make.

Don Green
Executive Director and CEO
The Napoleon Hill Foundation

FOREWORD

by Ruben Gonzalez

When Erik Swanson asked me to write the foreword to his latest #1 bestselling book in the series called *The 13 Steps To Riches on Organized Planning*, I was thrilled and honored, to say the least. Any chance to surround yourself with such leaders like Erik Swanson and also honor the classic work by the late, great Napoleon Hill, I jump at the opportunity. Erik has shared the stage with some of the top speakers from around the world, or should I say they have shared the stage with him. He has shown millions of people how to achieve their goals and dreams.

I've been competing in the luge on and off since 1986. Hurdling down an icy chute at 80-90 MPR. The luge is the only Olympic sport that's timed to the 1/1000th of a second. Everything counts— even your breathing counts. So we plan everything. We plan what we want to do and how to get out of trouble (contingency planning).

As a four-time Olympian in the sport of luge, I've had every coach I've ever had tell me, "Ruben, proper preparation prevents poor performance." I've had that concept drilled into me by coaches with Russian, Austrian, Romanian, Latvian, and even South Boston accents.

Everyone wants to win. Wanting to win is not enough. You have to be willing to prepare to win. In other words, you have to take the time to do your organized planning.

No matter how many times we've been to a particular luge track, we "walk the track" with Coach before we train on it.

No matter how long we have been traveling, no matter how tired we are, whether we've just ridden in a van for twelve hours from Innsbruck to Sarajevo or flown ten hours from Europe to Calgary before we go to the hotel, we walk the track.

We go to the top of the track, and for two hours, we literally walk down the track, slipping and sliding the whole way, planning exactly what lines we will take during training. Coach knows the best lines—he was World Champion three times. Coach knows the shortcut to success. We follow Coach and take detailed notes on everything he says.

Typically, it goes something like this; "OK, guys, this is curve three. You want to enter early. At this point, you want to be no more than three inches from the left wall. Over here, steer with a force of three (where zero is no steering and ten is all you've got). Down there at the expansion joint, give it a five, over there by that sign, hold it up, then at the end crank it with all you've got but remember to counter-steer or else you'll slam into the wall."

We feverishly write every word he says. Some of us even record Coach as he's talking. When we finally get to the hotel, we don't go straight to bed; we memorize the fastest lines and start visualizing our perfect run.

What if, on the way to the track, I had told Coach, "Coach, I'm not feeling well. Will you just drop me off at the hotel?"

Do you know what would happen? I'd take a hot shower, get a hot meal, snuggle under the warm covers, watch "Friends" or "Frazier" on TV in Serbo-Croatian while sipping a hot chocolate, and drift into a wonderful night's sleep, all the while thinking, "Those fools! They're freezing their rear ends out there!" And then the next day, I'd kill myself on the track and have only myself to blame.

Wanting to win is not enough. You have to prepare to win. Winners do whatever it takes to get to the next level. Are you willing to do whatever it takes? If you're not, then your dream is a pipedream.

This whole book is dedicated to the art of organized planning. Buy it, read it, underline the parts that resonate with you, write notes on the margins, discuss it with your coach or mentor, but most importantly, APPLY what you learn. Knowledge is not power. Applied knowledge is power.

You'll achieve your goals and dreams and make your life an adventure if you do. Make it an Olympic day!

RUBEN GONZALEZ

Ruben Gonzalez is a common man who achieved extraordinary things. He wasn't a gifted athlete. In school he was always the last kid picked to play sports. He didn't take up the sport of luge until he was 21. Four years and a few broken bones later, he was competing in the Calgary Winter Olympics. When he competed at the Vancouver Olympics at the age of 47, Ruben became the first person to ever compete in four Winter Olympics each in a different decade.

Ruben is a four-time Olympian and author of *The Inner Game of Success*. Since 2002 Ruben has spoken for over 100 of the Fortune 500 companies. His bestselling books have sold over 300,000 copies and have been translated to over 10 languages.

Ruben's incredible story takes people's excuses away and fills them with the belief and inspiration to face their challenges and fight for their goals and dreams.

www.TheLugeMan.com

Marie Diamond

ORGANIZED PLANNING BY A TRANSFORMATIONAL LEADER

In this chapter, I wish to go deeper into how you can Organize successful Transformational Leadership. I was inspired by the 10 major causes of failure in leadership and the 30 major causes of failure, both mentioned in the chapter Organized Planning in the book *"Think and Grow Rich"* by Napoleon Hill.

As a Master Teacher in the global phenomenon, *The Secret,* which was partly based on the knowledge of the book *Think and Grow Rich,* I want to change the wording used in Organized Planning. Using words like failure keeps the subconscious mind focused on attracting more failure. What you focus on is what you get more of.

Transformational leadership is the leadership style of the 21st century. These leaders are inspiring positive changes in their teams and their clients. They are concerned and involved in the business process but also focus on helping their team, their clients, and the planet.

Some of the most Valuable Sources of Success with Transformational Leadership are listed below:

Having a Purpose in Life

Transformational Leaders have a personal purpose, a purpose for their business, and a purpose of contributing to Humanity. When you have nothing to aim for, you will not be able to manifest a difference in your life on this planet.

Ability to Put Your Vision in a Detailed Plan

Transformational leaders are able to take their vision and surround themself with a team to create a detailed business and marketing plan. While the leader holds the vision, (s)he is able to guide his/her team to bring together the detailed plan for the implementation and manifestation of the vision.

Being the Best

Transformational Leaders are not focused on small numbers or small results because they always have a large vision and focus on the big impact of their products and services. As they know when they are the best in who they are and what they do, they will reach higher and wider than others. It is not ambition that drives them but a cause of changing the world in a positive way.

Heart of Service

Transformational Leaders bring forward products and services to make a difference to Humanity. Their heart is compassionate toward the planet and the suffering in Humanity. They will make a difference with ecological goods, planet-safe procedures, and create a diverse team around them, that supports each other. They are not asking this only from their team but use these values in every aspect of their leadership.

Gender Equality Remuneration

Transformational leaders pay their teams for the combination of services, solution-driven creativity, and leadership. Salaries and remuneration are not influenced by gender, race, religion, sexuality, cultural background, and other dismissive inequalities.

Inclusivity is Priority

Transformational Leaders are aware of the talents and skills of their team. They ask them to use this to fulfill their own purpose and the purpose of the business that they have joined. There is no top-down business decision model, but a model of listening to the team before decisions aligned with the vision are made.

Intuition and Imagination

Transformational Leaders are in touch with their gut feeling or their intuitive side thru spiritual practices. They are able to visualize the vision with their imagination. They are surrounded by a team that is allowed to listen to their intuition and have the ability to think outside of the box with their imagination.

Generosity

Transformational Leaders are generous in honoring the work of their team with positive conversations, financial rewards, and promotions. They know that recognizing the strength of their team is more important than getting themselves all the honors and awards.

Positive Attitude

Transformational leaders have a positive attitude toward their vision, goals, their team, and towards the future. They encourage others to have this positive attitude too. It helps the endurance and the vitality of the circle around them.

Loyalty

Transformational leaders are steadfast and focused on their vision and loyal to the team that supports them in building out their organization and manifesting their goals.

Encouragement

Transformational leaders are leading by example and encourage their team to do so too. There is no space for fear-based communication but only for encouraging others to be the best in who they are. Their conduct, sympathy, understanding, and fairness are a demonstration of their leadership skills.

Open Communication

Transformational Leaders are not focused on titles, educational degrees, and backgrounds but only on the human potential of their team. They communicate openly with them with always the vision and goals as a guiding star.

The Eternal Student

Transformational Leaders know that they never know enough about themselves, the world, and about leadership. They will always have a mentor, a teacher, a mastermind group, and books to guide them to learn more. Self-education never stops, and it is always with respect to the others. But it is more than education; it is applying as soon as you know the information so that your learning gives you results.

Mastering Your Emotions and Your Mind

Transformational Leaders do not lead by their ego. They have mastered their negative emotional reactions and thoughts or at least do not share them with their team. They reflect within before they have difficult conversations about team issues. Mastering Yourself is the key, or you will become the victim of your Ego.

Taking Care of Your Well Being

Transformational Leaders listen to their body as it is the vessel to manifest their vision with. Good sleep, an organic and healthy diet, regular exercise, daily walks in nature, meditation, and more contribute to your good health.

Keep Moving Forward

Transformational Leaders know that there is never a time that is right; it is time right NOW. Take everyday steps forward, and the journey will bring you to Success. Do not allow procrastination to dominate your life. When the Universe has given you a vision, you have the responsibility to fulfill this vision to the best of your abilities.

Persistence, Even Ehen Things Are Getting Though

Transformational Leaders keep their eye on the finish line: manifesting their vision. Of course, there can be difficult times, hardship, lack of money, legal issues, and so much more obstacles. But they will persist as they know there is the Light at the end of the tunnel.

Working and Living in a Positive and Harmonious Environment

Transformational leaders know that you need to have a harmonious and decluttered space around you. As a Feng Shui Master, I have been teaching this knowledge for more than 25 years. You can start this process by finding your Energy Number on my Free Marie Diamond App (Google play store and App store). Indicate your Gender and your birthday, and you will receive your Energy Number, four best compass direction, and video's how to start activating your office for Success and Abundance.

Picture Compass

Your home is the unconscious expression of yourself. When I enter a home or office, I always look for signs to see if people feel powerful. As you are the Universe within, you need to be in power in your life. When you are not in power, you are not attracting what you really desire. Instead, you will stay connected with a poor consciousness and feel vulnerable and weak. You will feel that you are the victim of your reality instead of being the master of your life.

European kings and queens to the emperors of China and all political leaders had one thing in common: they sought a long and powerful government. They wanted to be the masters of their countries.

Your life is like a country. Your wish is to be the master of yourself and to make your dreams come true. What can you change to become the master in your Universe? Here are your first steps.

STEP 1: Sit or sleep like a King or a Queen/ a President/ a Leader

Do you see the gifts of the Universe come to you, or do you sit with your back to them? At your home or workspace, you always need to see who enters, whether from your couch, dining table desk, or anything else you work on. Make sure you sit in such a way that you can see the incoming energy.

The Universe comes through the door and not through the windows. So facing a window and having your back towards the door is not efficient. The Universe walks in when you walk in. Even if you don't have any physical people walking in, you still come in, and you are the Universe.

You are not following the Principle of Power in the Universe when you come into your home and office and see:

In your living room, you are sitting with your back to the door, watching TV or talking to your family.

In your bedroom, when you wake up, you don't see the door immediately. In your office, you are sitting at a desk, but your back is facing the entrance of your office.

In a restaurant, your back is facing the entrance of the restaurant, or your back is facing the door when eating.

Solutions:

Rearrange your couches so you can see the door. Never have someone completely sitting with their back to the incoming flow of energy.

In your Bedroom: Place your bed on a wall so you can see your romantic partner coming in. When this is not possible, place a little mirror across the incoming door so you can see who is coming the moment you wake up.

In your Office/Workspace: Place your desk so you can see people walking in. When this is not possible, place a little mirror to the right or left and in front of you so that it shows you who is coming in from behind you.

Arrive first to your dinner appointment and make sure you can see the door and your guests arriving.

STEP 2: Be Supported by the Universe All the Time

When you consider kings, queens, and emperors, you realize they are always looking to be supported by a Higher Energy and by their people.

A king or queen will always sit on a throne that supports their back and their neck. Their arms are resting on the chair. You wish to have the same support.

A true Master of Transformation allows support from the Universe at all times because, without this support, you are unable to fulfill your dreams and manifest your true potential.

Successful people always sit on impressive high-backed chairs. They are not sitting on small chairs without back support.

You are not following the Principle of Power in the Universe when you come into your home and office, and you see

- You are sitting on a chair with a low back.
- You are sitting on a chair with slats.
- You are sitting on an old chair that is falling apart.
- You are sitting on the ground or on a pillow.
- You are sitting on a couch without support for your back.
- You are sleeping in a bed without a headboard or on a mattress on the ground.
- You are sleeping in a bed with metal or wooden slats.

Solutions:

Buy a high-backed chair and place it behind your desk, especially when your back is facing the door.

Cover the back of your chair with fabric or place a pillow between you and the back of the chair.

Remove the old chair and purchase a new one.

Place a headboard at the end of your bed to support your head, or start by placing pillows between your head and the wall.

Place your mattress on another mattress, on bricks, or anything that brings it 30 cm or a foot from the ground.

Cover the metal and wooden slats with fabric or place pillows against the slats.

When you can't do anything like this, make sure you place support behind you symbolically: a religious, spiritual, or philosophical image or statue of support: a Saint or Angel in the Christian tradition, an image of the Letters of God, an image of a Rabbi from the Jewish tradition, the Koran from the Muslim tradition, Gurus from the Hindu tradition, Images of

Gods or Goddesses, spiritual Teachers from other Eastern traditions, an image of the CEO or the president of your company, or just an image of a mountain (not completely covered by snow).

Place a rock, a Buddha statue, an image of an angel, or any other image of support connected with your religious, spiritual, or philosophical beliefs behind your home, opposite the front door.

You can also place a large, round-leaved plant behind you for support.

STEP 3: Surround Yourself with Power

The images/statues that are hanging around you represent you. The more powerful the images/statues that are in your home or office, the more you will be treated as a powerful person.

Depending on what you wish to accomplish and in what area you wish to be powerful, your images will be different.

When you wish to be a powerful scientist, then make sure you hang an image of Einstein or Newton in your living or working space.

When you wish to be an author, place books that have been read for hundreds of years; try Shakespeare.

Make sure you resonate with the images. If you don't like the person, don't hang it up.

What are Powerful Images?

- Images of successful people in your profession.
- Images of award-winning people connected with your goal.
- Images of your idols and heroes, dead or alive.
- Images of famous people.
- Images of mountains.
- Images of your masters, CEO, or managers.

- Images of your certificates.
- Images of Buddha, Jesus, Angels, Saints, or Gurus.
- Statues of (fake) awards like an Oscar with your name on it.
- Front covers with your image on them (even if fake).
- Images of your products in a golden frame.
- Images of royal or imperial figures.
- Images of people you admire.
- Images of your logos, ads, marketing material, articles.
- Your vision board with your success goals.

Where to Place Your Powerful Images?

Make sure you have powerful images at the entrance of your company Place them in the North area of your office.

You can hang them behind your chair to feel supported by powerful people.

You can also hang them in front of where you sit to focus on these successful people.

Place them in your personal success direction. Download the Free Marie Diamond App (for iPhone and smartphones available) and find out your personal energy number. You will immediately see with the Diamond Compass where your personal success direction is in the room you are standing in.

You can always place your Power affirmation in the north area of your living room, as it will impact all the people living in this home. Or you can place it in the north area of a conference room, and it will create power for the whole company.

STEP 4: Activate your personal Success Direction

You can also place more personal information about your Success and Abundance in your personal success direction. You can find your personal

Success direction in the Free Marie Diamond App and with some videos to help you with implementation.

Marie Diamond, Master Teacher in The Secret and Global Renowned Feng Shui master with more than 1 million online students.

www.MarieDiamond.com

Extra Tips:

Make sure there is no clutter at the entrance or in the North area of your office. Remove all images in your home that do not convey power or success.

MARIE DIAMOND

Marie Diamond is one of the world's top transformational leaders, speakers, and internationally bestselling authors. A renowned voice on Law of Attraction, Feng Shui, and Dowsing, Marie Diamond is the creator of the Diamond Feng Shui, Diamond Dowsing, and Inner Diamond Meditation Programs. A 'seer' in a modern context, Marie was the only European star featured in the worldwide phenomenon The Secret. Latest movies she contributes to are "Beyond The Secret" and "Thoughts become Things" in 2020.

Marie merges her profound intuitive knowledge of Energy and the Law of Attraction, with her extensive studies of Quantum Physics, Meditation, Feng Shui, and Dowsing to transform the success, financial situations, relationships, motivations, and inspirations of individuals, organizations, and corporations. Her clients include billionaires, A-list celebrities in film and music (Steven Spielberg, The Rolling Stones, Paula Abdul, etc.), top-selling writers, motivational speakers (Rhonda Byrne, Jack

Canfield, Bob Proctor, Marianne Williamson, Vishen Lakhiani, etc.), world-class athletes, leading CEOs, Fortune 500 Companies (BP-Amoco, Exxon Mobil, etc.), MLM Companies (Lyoness, WorldVentures, Nikken, Herbalife,etc.). Globally, Marie has assisted government leaders, and governmental organizations in Belgium, Kazakhstan, Russia, Iceland, USA, Canada, and Mexico by providing comprehensive advice and solutions based on her expertise.

Marie is a Founding Member of the Global Transformational Leadership Council and is both Founder and President of the Association of Transformational Leaders of Europe. Marie has established a world-class reputation for transforming the success, health, relationships, and spiritual wisdom for millions of people. She is someone that thousands of entrepreneurs, businesses, and corporations turn to for unique insights and guidance with branding, marketing, and business decisions. She is also knighted to Dame Commander for her contribution to Humanity.

www.MarieDiamond.com

Erik "Mr. Awesome" Swanson

BE CRYSTAL CLEAR

Napoleon Hill taught us the value of crystallizing our desires into action in the sixth step to riches by the use of what's called "Organized Planning."

Organized Planning is what I like to refer to as the 'glue' that brings your desires into action form. This is such a vital step in the process of your success. If missed, you are literally throwing away the blueprint that brings your desires and goals to fruition.

It's simply not enough to set your goals and desires and wish upon them coming true. So many people around the world try that method which to you and I seems incredibly ridiculous. After millions of people read the book *The Secret* when it came out back in 2006, a fair amount of them tried to simply 'imagine' their success. Lo and behold, it didn't work. They were missing the extremely vital step of setting their blueprint or organized plan.

Can you imagine being hungry and wishing for a juicy triple-decker cheeseburger? You close your eyes and imagine it in your mind. You wait five more seconds just to make sure you imagined it correctly. You then open your eyes, and voila… NADA!

This is how most people set up their game plan for their success. Unfortunately, it is not a great game plan. Trust me!

So, what is a great game plan?

Success Leaves Clues

One of the best lessons I learned early on in my career while working directly with the amazing Brian Tracy was the knowledge that success leaves clues. Brian would always remind me to seek out those individuals who were making a difference in the world, to seek out those super successful individuals who would either directly or indirectly mentor me. Why would I say directly or indirectly? Well, in this world, whether we like it or not, we are all mentors. We are all being watched by others. In fact, kids don't typically learn from parents with their parent's words. Instead, they learn from the actions their parents take.

So, if success truly does leave clues, then don't we owe it to ourselves to seek out successful individuals and follow in their footsteps by actually following in their footsteps?

I always love to remind myself and my coaching students that if you desire a certain, successful outcome, then seek out those who have tackled it before you and have succeeded. Seek out those people who are better than you in that particular area. For example, if I want to be a better chess player, I will learn and grow at a far more rapid pace by playing against people who are better than me in chess, rather than those whom I would normally dominate in the game. Such is the same in the game of life!

Winners Are All Around Us

There is a fantastic quote by Napoleon Hill that goes like this: "A Quitter never Wins—and—a Winner never Quits!" I love this quote because it's a constant reminder to always strive for your desired outcome. Those who never quit have such an advantage over those who have fantastic ideas, yet don't act upon them or only act upon them if it's easy to succeed.

I have a great friend who holds the record for being in four winter Olympics over four decades. His sport of choice was the Luge. I asked him how he decided to pick that sport since he lived in hot and humid

Houston, Texas. You don't really see too many winter sports being generated down in Texas! His answer floored me. He explained that he had a burning desire to be an Olympian. Nothing was going to get in his way of this. He knew that he would never give up, no matter what. In high school, kids used to call him 'Bulldog' because of his tenacity and determination. So, all that was left for him to do was pick a sport. He started researching each sport that could lead him into the Olympics. He started to notice that the Luge seemed to have the highest percentage of athletes who either were disqualified, dropped out, or quit. He said to himself, "Perfect!" He figured that if he knows he never quits, all he had to do was 'stick it out' longer than anyone else, and he would become an Olympian! That's exactly what he did.

That story always reminds me of another story Napoleon Hill mentions in *Think and Grow Rich*. Remember the story about Thomas Edison failing over 10,000 times before he figured out a way to make the incandescent light bulb? Can you imagine if he quit? We would all be left in the dark. Yes, pun intended. The point I'm making should be clear: success truly does leave clues, and your job is never to quit.

Create Your Own Ambassador's List

It's now time for you to create a list of highly successful individuals to whom you look up to. I call this "My Ambassador List." It's a list of individuals who I learn from. These people have all been successful in areas in which I strive to achieve the same or better results.

Don't be afraid to reach out to these highly successful individuals. From my experience, the most successful individuals who walk our earth are also the most accessible. This is one of their Habitude Warrior traits. Highly successful people do not achieve the highest level without being able to connect with others in such a great fashion. This is to your advantage as it makes it much easier to connect with them. They tend to be very open to mentoring people in the footsteps they took.

Leaders And Followers

Once you have established the relationships with those highly successful mentors, it's time to create the blueprint for your organized plan. It is up to you to watch, notice, learn, and take action upon the strategies your mentors had taught you by their actions to their successes. Remember, success leaves clues, so follow the leader.

In life, we have two types of people. We have Leaders, and we have Followers. Also in life, we choose to become either a Leader or a Follower or both at certain levels in our lives. It's important to establish yourself first as a Follower to learn the secrets of success from those who have mastered that in which you strive to be great at. But, don't stay there. Make a conscious choice and resolution to become a Leader once you have mastered those lessons and steps outlined by your mentors in which you followed. This is such a fantastic feeling once you have made that transition!

I remember when I made the transition in my speaking career. It's the story that I refer to as 'the time when Brian Tracy passed me the torch.' Wow! I was so excited for that day to arrive. I had been traveling for about seven years with Brian Tracy and the team, training groups around the world to become more successful in their businesses. Then, at the Javitz Center in New York City, in front of about 2,000 people in the crowd, Brian turns to me and waves me up to the stage, and hands me the microphone. This was one of the turning points in my life that assured me that I was moving into a leadership role in my career and in life.

It is your turn to transition into the new leader you were always destined to become. Lead the field and teach others by mentoring them to their success. Create your organized plan, stick with it and watch everyone soar around you, including YOU!

ERIK SWANSON

About Erik "Mr. Awesome" Swanson: As an Award-Winning International Keynote Speaker and 13 Time #1 Best-Selling Author, Erik "Mr. Awesome" Swanson is in great demand around the world! He speaks to an average of more than one million people per year. He can be seen on Amazon Prime TV in the very popular show SpeakUP TV. Mr. Swanson has the honor to have been invited to speak to many universities such as the University of California (UCSD), Cal State University, University of Southern California (USC), Grand Canyon University (GCU), and the Business and Entrepreneurial School of Harvard University. He is also a Faculty Member of CEO Space International and is a recurring keynoter at Vistage Executive Coaching. Erik also joins the Ted Talk Family with his latest TEDx speech called "A Dose of Awesome."

Erik got his start in the self-development world by mentoring directly under the infamous Brian Tracy. Quickly climbing to become the top trainer around the world from a group of over 250 hand-picked trainers, Erik started to surround himself with the best of the best and soon started to be invited to speak on stages alongside such greats as Jim Rohn, Bob Proctor, Les Brown, Sharon Lechter, Jack Canfield, and Joe Dispenza... just to name a few. Erik has created and developed the super-popular Habitude Warrior Conference, which has a two-year waiting list and includes 33 top-named speakers from around the world. It is a 'Ted Talk' style event that has quickly climbed to one of the top 10 events not to miss in the United States! He is the creator, founder, and CEO of the Habitude Warrior Mastermind and Global Speakers Mastermind. His motto is clear... "NDSO!": No Drama – Serve Others!

Author's Website: *www.SpeakerErikSwanson.com*
Book Series Website & Author's Bio: *www.The13StepstoRiches.com*

Jon Kovach Jr.

STANDARDS OF EXCELLENCE

If they come at all, Riches come in response to definite demands, based upon the application of definite principles, not by chance or luck.

~ Napoleon Hill, Think and Grow Rich

Planned or unplanned, calculated or uncalculated, the results and outcomes of everything are still part of a plan.

Every Great Story Begins With A Plan

As early as I can remember, I've always wanted to be a professional. That meant I wanted to be proficient at something enough to be sought after and highly regarded by others. Being a professional meant that I would be in a position to serve others using a skillset that I was confident, competent, and qualified to represent.

Throughout college, I focused on professional behaviors. I joined clubs and executive boards to learn and practice the proficiencies of experts. This desire awarded me experience getting published in significant news outlets and earning scholarships. They also helped me get elected to national leadership positions. The principles led me to be nominated and presented with national rankings and top leadership accolades in my future profession. I couldn't believe how easy it was to excel in the professional realm.

One of my favorite attributes of the pre-professional societies and organizations was how everyone focused on the same goal: to graduate with honors and land a great job in their most significant interests. Each student was so vibrantly supportive of each other's interests that it was easy to build friendships all over the globe. We'd travel to national and international conferences where we would network, learn more professional skills from experts, and make connections to further our love and passion for being professionals. It was the perfect environment for me to thrive. Although this pre-professional environment was fantastic, I was not prepared for the next step in the professional climb.

Now graduated and working for a great company, I was inspired to take the following steps in my profession by attending networking societies, organizations, and meetings. When I first attended, one of the organization's senior members asked me to get out of line for a speaking spot because I was too young to participate. He said, "You'll need to put in a few more years of tenure before anyone considers you for a speaking spot. So wait in line." In another event and national organized meeting I attended, I walked away with 30+ business cards in hand from strangers. Still, I had no clue who everyone was, what they did to serve others, and if I'd be speaking to them ever again. Instead, I walked out of that event feeling drained and treated like a money-bag target, and everyone wanted me to have their business. It was like a cheap car sales experience where I was sold anything and everything I didn't need, and nobody wanted to listen to me.

If You Fail To Plan, You Plan To Fail

The last meeting and group I attended sounded promising as they had measurements and statistics, giving credit and clout to its professional structure. It's like overnight, I became an inspector of professional groups with my notepad in hand, ready to see if these organizations passed code or something. After sitting through this professional meeting, I noted that they had structure and sequence. Still, my first impression was that this wasn't an organization that helped professionals build relationships. Instead, it was a referral community built on 30-second elevator pitches and a group of paying customers who all had needs and were trying to fulfill those needs from the same group of 30 people each week. I wasn't entirely against it, so I returned a few more times, and I even signed up as a member, only to be utterly disappointed in my results. It's as if everyone knows they need to network to grow their business, but they engage in only surface-level, transactional ways of thinking.

I thought networking was supposed to be about relationships. I thought professional relationships were all about serving others with the professional skillsets and proficiencies we had developed. And finally, I thought, and I guess I was wrong, that the point of professional networking was to surround yourself with people who were willing to work together with a common interest in seeing each other succeed. Those were the lessons I learned in my pre-professional organizations. Those were my beliefs in the "real professional world." It was so confusing, painful, and disheartening to realize my dreams of being a professional and sharing that in a community of believers, too, would have to be created rather than found.

Dissatisfied with the expected standards and frustrated with the results of almost all the networking groups, societies, and organizations, I set out on a mission to fix the way professionals network.

The Networkers Guide To Success

I believe that the formula to building valuable relationships in life and business is as easy as TAFFI, which includes:

Trust + Accountability + Follow Up + Fun + Investment = Valuable Relationships

I've always been a firm believer in two life-leading principles that have guided me to great relationships and endless opportunities. Those principles are:

1. **Start where you stand:** Start where you stand means there are no cheat codes or advantages in life, therefore is up to us to begin every journey from the present.

2. **Build from the ground up:** Building from the ground up means that if you believe you can do it better, start building. The right people and resources will present themselves as your vision becomes a reality.

I wanted to curate an environment for professionals to build powerful relationships that produced results. I knew that if I could re-educate professionals on the power of connection and then build trust, we'd be able to help them achieve their goals in networking. So I began marketing and broadcasting a free networking group to attract a local market of networking hungry professionals in the Salt Lake City area.

I would lead the group in a series of ice-breaker activities at these events. My intentions in these activities were to break down the guarded, emotional, and prideful walls in each person and build trust as fast as possible. I knew if I could get each attendee to smile, laugh, or share a quick story, I could get them to open up more to **trust** strangers in the room. Part of these ice breakers included sharing sequences of people focusing on the positive achievements they are experiencing in their lives. The weekly declarations and **accountability** shared between members made this group supportive and easy to **follow up** on success and progress.

We'd lead the ice-breaker activities into competitive team-based games. These competitive games were **fun** and engaging and helped each person act as themselves rather than as a representative of their business or organization. At this point, each group member would be open, willing, and even enthusiastic to support one another in their needs, insomuch that they would voluntarily give their knowledge, resources, and skillsets to help each other in the group—that's the **investment** part.

The last thing we'd do in these groups is we'd talk about our greatest needs and challenges, and the group members would offer up solutions in the form of PROFITS (which is an acronym that I will expound on in *The 13 Steps To Riches, Volume 9: Mastermind*). PROFITS are channels, modalities, and solutions that most professionals and business owners seek when networking with others—People, Resources, Opportunities, Funding, Information, Technology, Systems/Solutions, etc. These PROFITS were a collaboration with a colleague and mentor, Levi McPherson, who believed in a similar networking model.

After each exercise, we'd ask the members to take immediate action on the resources they received, and we would follow up with them at the next meeting. And after six months of following up with these professionals, we concluded that these simple networking, connecting, and building relationships led to an accumulated value of $20,000 transacted, earned, and raised amongst the 40-50 people regularly attending our networking event. The way we networked helped a small group of people make a lot of profits, and my 'free networking' event made $0 off of it all. That's when I knew we had created actual value for professionals, and they profited from our model.

A Champion's Standard of Excellence

After thoroughly reading through some of my favorite business and success classics, including *Think and Grow Rich* by Napoleon Hill, *How To Win Friends and Influence People* by Dale Carnegie, *The 7 Habits of Highly Effective People* by Stephen R. Covey, and *Never Eat Alone* by Keith Ferrazzi, I developed about 30 of my own personal "Mastermind Methodologies" to help professionals accelerate their successes and overcome their immediate challenges, which is what we used in our networking meetings.

I realized that I needed to take this methodology to market, thus, birthing the Champion Circle Networking Association. In this story, I always had a vision and a standard. My vision was to become a professional, and my standard from the beginning was to serve others. Hill stated in *Think and Grow Rich*, "Organized planning is the crystallization of desire into action, the sixth step to riches." Once your desires become concrete, every second of life thereafter becomes the planned or unplanned accumulation of events that lead to your goals and aspirations. Planning is inevitable, but organizing the journey by taking matters into your own hands will ultimately accelerate your plans for success.

JON KOVACH JR.

About Jon Kovach Jr.: Jon is an award-winning and international motivational speaker and global mastermind leader. Jon has helped multi-billion-dollar corporations, including Coldwell Banker Commercial, Outdoor Retailer Cotopaxi, and the Public Relations Student Society of America, exceed their annual sales goals. In his work as an accountability coach and mastermind facilitator, Jon has helped thousands of professionals overcome their challenges and achieve their goals by implementing his accountability strategies and Irrefutable Laws of High Performance.

Jon is the Founder and Chairman of Champion Circle, a networking association that combines high-performance-based networking activities and recreational fun to create connection capital and increase prosperity for professionals.

Jon is the Mastermind Facilitator and Team Lead of the Habitude Warrior Mastermind and the Global Speakers Mastermind & Masterclass founded by Speaker Erik "Mr. Awesome" Swanson.

Jon speaks on a number of topics, including accountability, The 4 Irrefutable Laws of High Performance, and The Power of Mastermind Methodologies. He is a #1 Best-Selling Author and was recently featured on SpeakUp TV, an Amazon Prime TV series. He stars in over 100 speaking stages, podcasts, and live international summits on an annual basis.

Author's website: *www.JonKovachJr.com*
Book Series Website & Author's Bio: *www.The13StepsToRiches.com*

Amado Hernandez

WHY ORGANIZED PLANNING DOESN'T WORK FOR ME

First comes thought, then organization of that thought, into ideas and plans; then transformation of those plans into reality. The beginning, as you will observe, is in your imagination.
~ Napoleon Hill

My planning is anything but organized because organized planning has never worked for me. I am probably in the minority because planning is a requirement for most people, an obsession for many, and a profession for some. There are family planners to help you start a family, and there are funeral planners to help you with final arrangements. In between, there are wedding planners and event planners for everything from a product launch to a grand opening to your dog's birthday party. The label financial planner is often misunderstood and certainly abused. And don't even get me started on business planners.

Although I have never used professional planners (for personal or business reasons), I recognize that they are quite the thing now. For example, a Google search of quinceañera planning returns over 8 million results. For those of you who are Latino or want to be or have ever been to a quinceañera, you know that it's a pretty big deal. And I wonder how much magic is lost by too much planning beyond the family traditionally gathering around the kitchen table. The magic is all about sharing stories about generations of quinceañeras and everyone passionately planning the next one. Perhaps the only ones that use professional quinceañera planners are fresas (you might have to look that up on Urban Dictionary). For the rest of us, it's up close and personal.

For DIY planners, there are books, apps, programs, and journals that have morphed way beyond the Franklin Covey organizers that were all the rage many years ago. Now they're as obsolete as a Rolodex. Some people plan, track, and record every detail of their lives ad nauseum wasting countless hours that they'll never recover. They're like The Beatles' *Nowhere Man*, "Making all his nowhere plans for nobody."

Whether you are planning a quinceañera or your road to a million, it all begins with a thought. Then, it all depends on your ability to visualize and organize your thoughts and transform them into reality. And finally, the magic is in the process more than it is in the end result.

Some people may need help from a professional planner, planning tools, or a combination of everything other than just digging in and making their own plans themselves. That doesn't include me. That type of organized planning has never worked for me. I know that from my personal experiences.

Half a lifetime ago, I was "on plan" for realizing "The American Dream." I was 31 and married with four children. I was an engineer at Rockwell with a big office and a bigger 401k. Then it happened! A friend gave me a copy of a book by A.L. Williams titled *Common Sense: A Simple Guide for Financial Independence*. When I was reading that little red book, I discovered Napoleon Hill and *Think and Grow Rich*.

Reading *Think and Grow Rich* was the "aha moment," an "epiphany," and a "wake-up call" that initiated a paradigm shift in my life. It quickly dawned on me that "rich" could mean much more than my bank account and retirement plan. Before that, my "plan" was to work in aerospace until I could retire with a fat pension and then "live the life." My goal was to become the first Latino Vice President at the company, which would give me a big corner office, a company American Express Card, a Buick, and comfy retirement.

But a corner office, AmEx, and Buick were not what I wanted. Napoleon Hill convinced me that I was better than that. Much better. My plan changed big time! Suddenly it wasn't about money. It was about making an impact. I made a conscious decision to be able to educate people and empower them to live their lives the way they dreamed about. And to do that, I had to have a plan.

Some people make plans so detailed that there is no room for error - that there is no flexibility. Their plans are kind of like a paint-by-the-numbers kit. It's all there for you. Paints, brushes, and (wait for it) a canvas having outlines with numbers matching numbers on individual paint containers. But do you know what you get when you finish your painting? You get exactly what you should have expected. Why? Because there was no magic from the get-go. You didn't pick out the canvas, brushes, or paints. All you did was decide on a finished painting that yours would never look like. So you set yourself up for failure before your first brush stroke.

Don't live your life like a paint-by-the-numbers kit. Instead, pick out your own brushes and paints and start with a completely blank canvas. In Latin, it's tabula rasa ("scraped tablet" or "clean slate"). The theory of tabula rasa is that we are all born without built-in mental content; that all knowledge comes from personal experiences and perception. What does that tell you about having someone else make your plans for you?

I NEEDED A PLAN when I decided to forget about VP title, corner office, AmEx card, and Buick. But I wasn't going to find it in a paint-by-numbers kit. So, one day, I sat down with a new legal pad and the gold Cross pen they gave me when I left Rockwell. I invested a couple of hours and created my own 5-point plan. Here it is:

1. Fatten thy purse.
2. Prospect for people and for business.

3. Reward yourself for all your great activities.
4. Be simple-minded.
5. Have dates and deadlines for the above-noted projects. (Milestones)

My planning process is internal, like a GPS navigation system. At any given time, I have destinations and ETAs. And, at any given time, I can not only react to roadblocks but, more importantly, anticipate them and make necessary course adjustments.

Thank God, we're all different. Paint-by-numbers plans may work for some people, but even the thought of it takes away all of the fun and excitement for me. Iconic actress Bette Davis (you know her - the one with the "Bette Davis" eyes) once said, "Fasten your seat belts; it's going to be a bumpy ride." So bring it on. I love bumpy rides. And I'm never going to do any painting by the numbers.

So what's the plan for organized planning? Like Napoleon Hill said: "The beginning, as you will observe, is in your imagination." Everything starts with a thought, a dream. I believe that the emphasis should not be on planning. The magic is not in planning; it is in making it happen. Visualize what you want and do whatever it takes to make it happen. If you need a formal or written plan, keep it short and simple, and create it yourself. And don't forget that plans (like rules) are meant to be changed and sometimes ignored.

The next time you plan a quinceañera or new business venture, think about how much time and energy you want to invest in planning and how much time and energy you want to invest in execution making it happen. No matter how carefully you might plan something, something will probably go wrong with it. Expect that. It's okay. With your experience, passion, and commitment, you'll finesse your way through it and enjoy every bump along the way. I'll leave you with a proverb adapted from 18th Century poet Robert Burns: "the best-laid plans often go astray." And that's why organized planning has never worked for me.

AMADO HERNANDEZ

About Amado Hernandez: Amado was born in Mexico of humble beginnings and raised in Los Angeles, California. As an avid reader, Amado always focused on self-development. He coaches sales professionals to make six and seven figures in real estate.

Amado believes in a progressive culture, one people-centric where clients' dreams come true and salespeople thrive; at the end of the day, we all want to be respected and pursue our happiness.

My goal is to leave a legacy-making a difference in people's lives.

With 33 years of Real Estate experience, Mr. ABC Amado Hernandez successfully operates and grows his Excellence Empire Real Estate Moreno Valley office. Broker/Owner Amado first opened his doors in 1995, and Excellence currently has over 60 offices in Southern California, Las Vegas, Merida Yucatan, Mexico, and over 1,000 Agents. He is also part owner of a highly successful Mortgage company Excellence Mortgage and owner of Empire Escrow Services. Mr. Amado is also involved with his community and currently serves as Director at Inland Valley Association of Realtors and will be the President-Elect for 2023. Amado serves as a Director of CAR (California Association of Realtors).

Author's Website: *www.ExcellenceEmpireRE.com*
Book Series Website & Author's Bio: *www.The13StepstoRiches.com*

Angelika Ullsperger

CHAOS TO CLARITY

"No one plans to fail, but some forget to plan."

Growing up in a very chaotic environment, I got used to chaos. It became comfortable. For longer than I can remember, my organization method was no organization. I would avoid planning at all costs because I was accustomed to chaos. If I were okay with the chaos, it wouldn't cause stress. At the time, it worked. As far as progressing in life, this is not an ideal plan of attack by any means. The chances are that disorganization and chaos will not take you far in life. I have learned a lot about organized planning in my personal development journey. I had to because the chaos was no longer supporting me. My disdain for structure caused me to miss out on opportunities. I struggled to keep up with anything and everything. I watched my responsibilities pile up as I struggled to accomplish my plans. Even basic household tasks became stressful. To this very day, if I stop making time to prepare, I instantaneously begin to lose track, and my plans begin to unravel. It took me years of constantly missing out on opportunities and special moments with loved ones to realize that organization and planning were vital for success.

If you really want to get somewhere, do you need a plan? You don't go on a road trip to a specific destination, just hoping that the roads you take will get you there. The easiest way to figure out what roads you need to take is by figuring out the destination. That's one of the most important parts of organized planning is figuring out the end goal.

Take a minute as you read to consider, "What is my end goal?"

As you consider the end goal, I will start at the beginning. Before you do any important thinking, you need a blank canvas in your mind. I would recommend going somewhere quiet where you can be alone. Make sure to have a pen and paper nearby in case important thoughts pop up. Close your eyes and relax. I use 'square' breathing, a pattern of in-hold-out-hold, four seconds each, four times. A good breathing technique can slow down your heart rate and decrease your stress. Once you are present, your mind is free from cluttered thoughts. You now have ample space to think. This is a great way to begin constructing a plan. Now, you're ready.

Write down anything that comes to you when your head is filled with things to get done, people to talk to, obligations to fulfill, and it gets hard to keep track and think clearly. One benefit of writing everything out is that we don't have to worry about Miller's Law. The law states that an individual can hold on to an average of seven active thoughts in one moment.

Picture a juggler with seven bright red balls. Each ball represents a different thought in the forefront of your mind. In your hands sit three additional balls (thoughts) you want to consider, so you toss them in rotation. One problem, the juggler can only juggle a maximum of seven balls, so three random balls get dropped and roll off out of sight. However, the juggler is still focused on tossing seven balls, so they forget about the three that leave the rotation and roll-off.

If you can only have about seven thoughts at a time, it will be significantly less effective to plan in your head. When you let your ideas flow through you onto the paper and out of your head, you make room to keep thinking. As a result, you won't forget your ideas, AND you can reference and plan with the ideas you've already written down.

So what is your end goal? Work backward from there.

For your life, your projects, your hobbies. For whatever goal you are working towards, figure out what steps need to be taken to reach your goal. Break it down into smaller sub-goals/milestones. Even better, break each sub-goal down into action steps. For greater clarification, there is the option to keep breaking each item down until everything has a place. Simple yet thorough enough to create a clear path to the vision ahead. By outlining a path, you get clarity and know why you're getting up each day. You can make sure you are doing everything you need to without forgetting important steps. Proper planning and organization will nature drive and discipline. It's always easier to take action when you have a roadmap for your destination.

It is, however, important to remember that life is a fluid, beautiful adventure yet unpredictable. Often things don't go as planned. Therefore I must also stress the importance of having flexibility with your planning. Events out of your control time are an unstoppable force, so think about fluffing it up with that). Reassessing your goals due to changing circumstances will be commonplace and natural. Don't be so set in your plans that you cannot adjust them when a problem arises. Formulate a solid plan but don't be afraid to change aspects of the plan; sometimes, that's part of the planning process. Just because obstacles pop up doesn't mean you can't make it to your destination. There is a myriad of different paths to advance towards a goal.

My favorite way to contribute to the process of getting organized is through a mind map. What's great about this? Everything! There's no wrong way to do it, as long as you do it. Grab a piece of paper, a whiteboard, notebook, giant sticky note, or whatever you prefer, and get ready to write. Depending on the type of planning I'm doing, or if I want to have a more thorough understanding of my plan, I will use more than one medium.

I love mindmaps so much that I use them in several ways. My system is usually to think first and organize second. Get everything that comes to your mind out, so you don't forget anything as a multitude of ideas keeps coming. You can't plan without ideas.

I use one strategy to list everything that comes to mind, making sure I leave a chunk of space at the top of the paper. Here, I will draw a horizontal line from one side to the other, which becomes a timeline. Next, I draw lines from the parts of my list upwards onto the timeline. It's a necessity for me to use brainstorming techniques like mindmaps, lists, or diagrams to create an organized plan. Finally, I include other elements to organize parts of my plans.

Make Lists

Create and use different shapes as bullets to group or create a hierarchy of your thoughts

---

|Group thoughts, concepts into different shapes | ← symbols work too

| (and sub shapes) |

*By adding visual elements, your eyes can separate and better process the information.

You could even learn to write in italics or have a second thicker pen to emphasize different techniques and specific plans for your needs. You could create a page for business meetings and deadlines. Maybe have a page specifically for your family's obligations and appointments. I have to use a page or two to write out goals, sub-goals, and action steps. Depending on your need for flexibility, you can use scissors, cut some pieces, and reorganize. If that's too much, you can just use some sticky notes or go online. In addition to making them, you can buy templates online or in some stores. Everything I discussed can be done digitally, but writing it down helps process and remember information. It leads to solid, structured plans. As a bonus, you can display them as a reminder.

This culmination of these ideas grew together into a personalized journal that I can change as I progress through life. One day I hope to share my creation so others can benefit as well. In the meantime, I use it to create plans and stay on top of them. All the planning in the world won't work if you don't keep up with it. After your phone is away and you are preparing to sleep, reference your plans and note what needs to be done tomorrow.

Every book in this series can be seen as a skill you can always develop and improve on. We all have different strengths and weaknesses, but there is something to learn from every book. Test out some of the various author's systems mentioned in the book, research additional systems, and find a mix of what works for you. You can be as detailed or simple as you desire. Just do it. The only way to fail is by not doing it at all.

"If You Fail to Plan, You Are Planning to Fail"
~ Benjamin Franklin

ANGELIKA ULLSPERGER

About Angelika Ullsperger: Angelika is a serial entrepreneur from Baltimore, Maryland. She is a fashion designer, model, artist, photographer, and musician. Angelika has extensive and well-rounded professional experience having worked as a business owner, carpenter, chef, graphic designer, manager, event planner, sales and product specialist, marketer, and coach. Angelika is now a #1 Best-Selling Author in the historic book series, *The 13 Steps To Riches.* She is a life- long learner with a sincere and genuine interest in all things of the world with a major interest in the formal subject of abnormal psychology, neuroscience, and quantum physics.

Angelika prides herself as someone who has saved lives as a friend, first responder, EMT, and knowledgeable suicide prevention advocate. With a vast knowledge and experience in multiple professions, Angelika is also a proud honorable member of Phi Theta Kappa, The APA, the AAAS, and an FBLA (Future Business Leaders Association) Business Competition Finalist. She is Certified in basic coding and blockchain technology. Amongst the careers and vast experience, Angelika is an adventurer and avid dog lover.

Her ultimate goals and dreams are to make a lasting positive impact in people's lives through her wealth of knowledge and skillsets.

Author's Website: *www.Angelika.world*
Book Series Website & Author's Bio: *www.The13StepstoRiches.com*

Dr. Anthony M. Criniti IV

PLAN YOUR WAY OUT OF THE GREAT PANDEMIC DEPRESSION

Think and Grow Rich by Napoleon Hill is one of the best classic books to teach someone how to become a financial success (as well as a success in other areas of life). In there, you will find his thirteen steps to riches; each one has its own separate chapter and analysis. The subject of our book is to interpret his sixth step to riches: organized planning. Let's review some of the major key highlights of this chapter.

Chapter 6 is the longest and one of my favorite chapters, with so much knowledge from so many different areas. It also serves as a historical snapshot of the Great Depression, which was the era when this book was written. Although Hill discussed various subjects, his main purpose in this chapter was to teach many people who were experiencing the tremendous pain of the Great Depression that you need organized planning to succeed. He was also offering a glimpse of hope to those who had plans that had fallen apart right in front of their eyes, probably due to the economic conditions that they had no control over.

Ironically, almost one hundred years later, reading this chapter gave me this eerie feeling as if he was speaking directly to the people alive today during the Great Pandemic Depression. Hill states: "The most intelligent man living cannot succeed in accumulating money—nor in any other undertaking—without plans which are practical and workable. Keep this fact in mind and remember that when your plans fail, temporary defeat is not permanent failure. It may only mean that your plans have not been sound. Build other plans. Start all over again" (Hill, 2011, p. 158).

Hill went on to offer encouragement to those suffering from failed plans by exemplifying how many times one of the greatest inventors had failed to create his most precious invention. "Thomas A. Edison "failed" ten thousand times before he perfected the incandescent electric light bulb. That is—he met with temporary defeat ten thousand times before his efforts were crowned with success" (Hill, 2011, p. 158). That is right, not 3,000 or 5,000 times as so many people confuse this number with being Edison had 10,000 failures to get it right.

Hill also had some really great quotes that I think are important to note. Here are two on mindset and success. First, Hill says: "No man is ever whipped until he quits—in his own mind" (Hill, 2011, p. 159). Until that person consents, he or she is still in the fight. Second, he states: "If you give up before your goal has been reached, you are a "quitter." A quitter never wins— and—a winner never quits" (Hill, 2011, p. 160). Finally, here is an awesome quote on money: "Some people foolishly believe that only money can make money. Money, of itself, is nothing but inert matter. It cannot move, think, or talk, but it can "hear" when a man who desires it, calls it to come" (Hill, 2011, p. 160)!

Chapter 6 also had an incredible analysis of leadership. Hill points out that people have two major roles when discussing leadership (both are very important): followers and leaders. He also highlights that each role has its time and place. He says: "Most great leaders began in the capacity of followers. They became great leaders because they were intelligent followers" (Hill, 2011, p. 161). I would add that all great leaders began as followers, especially because they need to be the first to follow the group they are leading. If leaders do not follow behind the movement they are leading, and they are only leading to a place called "Nowhere." This point was reinforced by Hill's list of eleven major leadership attributes.

I give Hill the highest kudos in this chapter for recognizing one of the major conclusions in my books: the vital importance of economics and finance. Hill says: "There is a principle known as the law of economics! This is more than a theory. It is a law no man can beat. Mark well the name of the principle, and remember it, because it is far more powerful than all the politicians and political machines" (Hill, 2011, p. 207). Similarly, when discussing the significance of economics in *The Necessity of Finance*, it was emphasized: "All of a nation's hard-earned wealth may be lost in an instant if its leaders neglect to implement intelligent actions learned from economics" (Criniti, 2013, p. 68). Hill knew the value of economics extremely well—he watched how economic leaders of his time destroyed immense wealth through their reckless decisions.

Another important conclusion from Chapter 6 was the significance of money and capitalism. He gives an example of the benefits of capital through an illustration of a simple breakfast for a New York family at a cheap price of a dime each. He breaks down how this meal could only be quickly provided at that price through an efficient capitalistic system. Hill states: "Stated briefly, the capitalists are the brains of civilization because they supply the entire fabric of which all education, enlightenment, and human progress consists of. Money, without brains, always is dangerous. Properly used, it is the most important essential of civilization" (Hill, 2011, p. 202). This point is spot on with a conclusion from my second book. As stated in Principle 128 of *The Most Important Lessons in Economics and Finance*: "Civilizations that use money require it for survival" (Criniti, 2014, p. 160).

Another crucial conclusion of this chapter involves self-control. The following quote is so important that I urge you to write it down and tape it to your bathroom mirror because it could change your life. Hill says: "5. Lack of self-discipline. Discipline comes through self-control. This means that one must control all negative qualities. Before you can control conditions, you must first control yourself. Self-mastery is the hardest job you will ever tackle. If you do not conquer yourself, you will be conquered by yourself. You may see at one and the same time both your best friend and your greatest enemy by stepping in front of a mirror" (Hill, 2011, p. 186).

Self-control is so important for survival and prosperity that I discussed it in various sections of my third book. I took Hill's statement one giant leap forward and emphasized that it is also needed to save our species and our planet. From The Survival of the Richest: "Finally, this sixth mass extinction can end another way…quietly. Humanity can realize the truths of our predicament and proactively do something about it. We can take care of our planet better while striving for unity and peace. We must use the same determination and energy level to resolve the current human predicament that we have used to create it. That is, we must exert as much control over our destiny as we have done over the rest of reformed nature. Self-control is a major part of our solution" (Criniti, 2016, p. 446)!

There were some other great conclusions from Chapter 6 that we don't have the space to explore deeply. These include an analysis of the thirty major causes of failure, the permanent substitution of the "go-giver" instead of the "go-getter," and leadership-by-consent as a more effective method over forced leadership. Hill also clears up the exact intention of the book: "The purpose of this book—A purpose to which I have faithfully devoted over a quarter of a century—is to present to all who want the knowledge, the most dependable philosophy through which individuals may accumulate riches in whatever amounts they desire" (Hill, 2011, pp. 204-205).

Finally, it was pleasing to find that Hill did spend time highlighting the significance of a purpose, although he never actually included it as a step to riches. Hill says: "2. Lack of a well-defined purpose in life. There is no hope of success for the person who does not have a central purpose or definite goal at which to aim. Ninety-eight out of every hundred of those whom I have analyzed had no such aim. Perhaps this was the major cause of their failure" (Hill, 2011, p. 185).

In conclusion, Chapter 6 was filled with a variety of golden nuggets that could help you build the skills needed to become a financial success. Hill taught about the qualities of leaders and failures, the need for self-control, the importance of having a purpose, and, my favorite: the necessity of economics, finance, and money. Nevertheless, the arching theme behind all of these different microlessons was to demonstrate that you need to have an organized plan to make a success out of your dreams.

As stated in Principle 216 of *The Most Important Lessons in Economics and Finance*: "Failure to plan is a highly probable plan to fail" (Criniti, 2014, p. 250). For readers stuck in the mud during these horrible economic times, there is a chance that you can play and win the lottery tonight. However, realistically, you have better odds of coming out on top if you immediately create and implement a highly organized plan. This is the more effective way to fight your way out of your current predicament and, ultimately, this ugly Great Pandemic Depression.

Bibliography

Criniti, Anthony M., IV. 2013. *The Necessity of Finance: An Overview of the Science of Management of Wealth for an Individual,* a Group, or an Organization. Philadelphia: Criniti Publishing.

Criniti, Anthony M., IV. 2014. *The Most Important Lessons in Economics and Finance: A Comprehensive Collection of Time-Tested Principles of Wealth Management.* Philadelphia: Criniti Publishing.

Criniti, Anthony M., IV. 2016. *The Survival of the Richest: An Analysis of the Relationship between the Sciences of Biology, Economics, Finance, and Survivalism.* Philadelphia: Criniti Publishing.

Hill, Napoleon. 2011. *Think and Grow Rich.* United Kingdom: Capstone Publishing Ltd.

DR. ANTHONY M. CRINITI

About Dr. Anthony M. Criniti IV: Dr. Anthony (aka "Dr. Finance®") is the world's leading financial scientist and survivalist. A fifth generation native of Philadelphia, Dr. Criniti is a former finance professor at several universities, a former financial planner, an active investor in diverse marketplaces, an explorer, an international keynote speaker, and has traveled around the world studying various aspects of finance. He is an award winning author of three #1 international best-selling finance books: *The Necessity of Finance* (2013), T*he Most Important Lessons in Economics and Finance* (2014), and *The Survival of the Richest* (2016). As a prolific writer, he also frequently contributes articles to *Entrepreneur, Medium,* and *Thrive Global.* Dr. Criniti's work has started a grassroots movement that is changing the way that we think about economics and finance.

Author's website: *www.DrFinance.info*
Book Series Website & Author's Bio: *www.The13StepsToRiches.com*

Barry Bevier

FAILING TO PLAN IS PLANNING TO FAIL

I recently read a true story about an airline pilot that couldn't fit his cup of tea into the cupholder in the cockpit, so he sat it on the center console. During the flight, the plane hit turbulence, spilling the drink onto the control panel and shutting off one engine. After the crew attempted an unsuccessful engine restart, the aircraft was diverted to a nearby airport and landed safely. When it happened again two months later to a crew from a different airline, the manufacturer realized there was a problem. Even though the plane cost $300 million, a tiny detail like cupholders being too small had a significant impact. This seemingly small oversight led to some harrowing moments. Fortunately, both flights were able to land safely, without injury to any of the passengers or crew or damage to the aircraft. Even though the detail of the cockpit may not have been planned out perfectly, there was a well-laid out plan of action that was put into play by the pilots to land the plane safely in the event of an engine failure.

It's interesting to me how people, including myself, fit or don't fit planning into our lives. Many of us spend more time planning a vacation than our annual or lifetime finances. Many couples spend more time planning their wedding than what their life together will be like. Many spend more time planning a day hike or bike ride than lifelong health goals. Napoleon

Hill's quote, "Plan your work and work your plan," reminds me of taking scuba diving lessons in San Diego several years ago. At the beginning of every class, the instructor would always say, "Plan your Dive, Dive your Plan…or Die". Perhaps a bit extreme, yet it brought out the importance of having a plan and carrying it out. It made a lot of sense to novice divers who often had more than just a little bit of trepidation over going underwater for long periods.

"Success comes to those who plan, to those who prepare, to those who are persistent, and to those who are willing to endure pain to achieve their goals" (Pastor John Hagee). When we fall in love with the dream, the plan becomes a necessary tool to acquire the desired outcome. Napoleon Hill said that plans must be realistic, practical, and not over complicated. In formulating a plan, several minds are better than one because they can look at the plan from a different angle and provide input to the plan that we may not have otherwise seen. (This is the concept of a Mastermind, the topic of future Volume 9 in this series).

In devising a plan, we don't anticipate failure, yet it's a good idea to plan for it or anticipate the need to adjust it for unanticipated conditions. As you take action on the plan, reviewing the progress and changing the plan to meet the goal is essential. Not only may obstacles occur, but opportunities may also arise that weren't considered in the original plan. Adjusting the plan to incorporate the new opportunities may achieve a better result. I like what Simon Sinek said, "Always plan for the fact that no plan ever goes as planned."

I have incorporated at least some level of planning in many of the things I've done in my life. I've learned through both good and bad experiences, the importance of planning and changing the plan where appropriate or necessary.

Throughout my life, my personal plans changed a lot. In 2000, I married my soulmate, Linda. We had dreamed about and planned for a long, fruitful, fun-loving life together. Although she had a debilitating autoimmune disease, our life was abundant and full of blessings. However, those plans changed abruptly ten years after we were married when she became very ill and passed away from a combination of her disease and the side effects of the medications she had been taking for over twenty years. Our plan was out the window, and I had to think about and plan what I desired my life to look like without her.

At the time, I was fully engaged in my engineering profession and had not anticipated any changes during the rest of my career. However, a few years after her passing, I became disenchanted with the engineering profession. I was more and more driven to find a new career where I could help people improve their health and avoid what happened to my family. It took a while to determine exactly what my new mission in life was and develop a plan to carry it out. A plan that could be helpful to others, as well as provide economic stability for my daughters and me. Even after I had a plan for that overall concept and started to put it into play, it seemed like I was constantly changing. It changed as I learned more, found other opportunities, and realized where I could help people the most in their health and wellness journey. I spent a lot of time thinking what my new goals would be. Then, I realized that I wasn't clear in my vision.

Brian Tracy said, "A clear vision, backed by definite plans, gives you a tremendous feeling of confidence and personal power." As I went through my journey, I finally discovered my vision. Even then, I still lacked the confidence and power that I could make a change and be successful. It was only after the vision became crystal clear that I could see where I was headed and developed the confidence that I could be successful. After I started to put the plan into play, I started feeling the power that motivated me and drove me forward every day, doing the activities required to achieve my goal.

Plans are absolutely useless until action is taken to carry out the plan and reach the goal. I used to have a propensity to overthink and procrastinate taking the necessary action to put the plan in motion. And especially if the plan did not directly involve others taking action too. Since a plan can always be changed, there comes a time when getting started just needs to happen. Abraham Lincoln said, "Give me six hours to chop down a tree, and I'll spend the first four sharpening the ax." While we need to spend enough time to develop a good plan, it doesn't need to be perfect, perhaps not even complete. A good plan put into action now is always better than any perfect plan that is never put into play. I know; I've done it. Life is so much more fun and successful when you just take action.

BARRY BEVIER

About Barry Bevier: Barry Bevier is a proud father of two amazing daughters in their mid-twenties, who are pursuing their passions in psychology and architecture in Southern California. He was raised on a family farm near Ann Arbor, Michigan. Growing up, he developed his faith in God, a strong work ethic, a love for nature, and a passion to help others. After completing his master's degree in civil engineering at the University of Michigan, he pursued a career in engineering, which eventually brought him to Southern California.

In 2000, he married the love of his life, Linda. They shared a beautiful life for ten years, until she succumbed to the effects of lupus and 20 years of treatment with prescription medications. Since then, Barry pivoted his career path into educating and helping others. Barry has educated himself in alternative, natural modalities in wellness and became a Licensed Brain Health Trainer through Amen Clinics. He also works with a new technology in stem cell supplementation that releases your own stem cells.

Author's Website: *www.BRBevier.Stemtech.com*
Book Series Website & Author's Bio: *www.The13StepstoRiches.com*

Bonnie Lierse

ORCHESTRATED ORGANIZATION

There is an excitement and an exhilarating feeling when you start with an outstanding plan and organize it!

It takes a certain personality to be excessively organized; however, I do believe we all need balance! Do you feel balanced?

I have studied numerous personality types over the years, and there are so many variations of "personality tests." Certainly, I know an "analytical" personality comes into play with organization and planning! My real estate partner, Dana, is definitely that way. She is a great balance for me. I'm the extreme opposite. For me, it's a learned skill I am still working on! It does NOT come easy! However, my strengths are determination, focus, and the extraordinary desire for success! I know my passion and my "WHY"! (That's KEY, by the way!) That is a huge advantage! When I cannot organize or plan something on my own, I'll reach out to people that DO have those strengths and get advice! It's called DELEGATION, as in my "Volume 4" book series!

My daughters are the perfect example of people who organize and plan everything! It's a fantastic quality!

I absolutely love stretching myself outside my comfort zone. Just kick away the box! Balance is one of my stronger beliefs! It takes time and practice to become balanced in the four personality types!

When I started my "interior accessory design" business years ago, my goal was to become a DIRECTOR with this business. Focus and passion were a priority, but as I built a large team, I had to lead by example and get organized through planning! You better believe that I reached my goal through organized planning. By the time I gave birth to my son and first-born Brandon, I became a director after one and a half years in my business. (By the way, that was considered super quick to become a director). I could have come up with many excuses why I couldn't reach that goal, but I soared through, despite obstacles you'll learn about in the next few book chapters.

Recently, I started journaling. I always planned on journaling, but my follow-through wasn't there! It has taken a major change, plan and shift in my thought process & life to start pretty "consistent" journaling! I'm truly excited about it. It is part of being organized and takes some super planning and follow-through (There are some sensational calendars out there to help stay organized.)!

It took my husband Tommy, my best friend and soulmate who passed recently, for me to wake up to "time is precious and is going fast"! He was extremely, extremely organized and planned everything! I'm definitely lost without him! I loved his perspective. Every detail was in his calendar or on pieces of paper in his pocket! He definitely had a system. He was also very driven by his passions! Running his websites took being organized and allowing time for it! Priorities are crucial! I knew he had my back as well!

Now is the time to be efficient! Get things done, and the only way is to have an organized plan! It's almost exciting to be open to learning these skills about being organized and planning! Difficult to have such success without it or someone else's support! If you can learn to delegate what you are WEAK at, the world will change for you! Just don't be afraid to ASK for help! There are many virtual assistants out there!

Yes, being part of a leadership and mentorship group was a big factor in my changes and was very eye-opening, including "Leadership Team Development" and "Habitude Warriors." I'm also part of a leadership group in real estate, "Bridges Business Solutions" and "Pearson Smith Realty."

I am extremely open to constantly stretching and growing myself from the inside out. You cannot miss it when you are getting it from all sides! Change starts within us, and being open to improving and stretching!

Organized planning only comes naturally to some, not everyone! I have to really focus on it and work at it!

When I went to Pratt Institute (art school), it was imperative to be organized and plan or my projects wouldn't have gotten done quickly! Lots of late nights!

Even writing these books takes time planning and staying organized with time! (Trust me when I say I'm not perfect and can miss a deadline)! But, when you love doing something, it flows and comes easier!

What is amazing to me is that we all can evolve from where we are to where we want to be if we are open to comprehending our strengths and weaknesses! So admit where you need the help and, most important, ASK for it!

Even planning a big trip takes organization from planning the trip like our cruise, packing, etc. When you take many business trips as I do, you'll understand it's vital!

From my friend Mel Mason and my daughter Cassi, I learned that you need to declutter yourself, your mind, and your life to become organized. It takes a plan and then truly working the plan.

I watch my children Cassi and Jared, Viktoria, and Brandon, and how they have to be so super organized with their lifestyles with their children and my delicious grandchildren! Sometimes, it takes even a colorized, sticky note calendar. Kids can always throw wrenches into plans! Be ready for any surprise, good or not so good.

Sometimes, planning doesn't always work out.

After losing my husband three months ago, my first puppy, Diamond, and now I just lost my second puppy, Molly, this week, which was a big mental wrench! That certainly was not in my plan at all! We do our best to plan but sometimes get hit with lots of curveballs! You better get up quick, though, and not stick your head in the sand! It's okay to feel sad for a bit, but you need to keep moving forward.

Recently, I was invited onto a "Divine Dynasty" with Jessa Carter! This was not in the plan, but I'm blessed it was presented on my beautiful, spectacular journey! It's been an eye-opening awakening!

We never know what miracles and magic will be put on our path to develop us and bring us to the next stage in our lives! I love surprises, so I am fantastic with the unexpected!

Organization has its place, but we are always thrown a wrench into it at times!

My belief is to be ready for what was NOT in the plan! Sometimes, that's better than what was in the plan.

I get thrilled about "conquering" the fear of planning! (Because it does not come naturally to me) It's so not my nature that it actually excites me. I love being challenged. Time management falls under planning and works hand and hand with that! The better you are with time management, the better you can lay out your plan! That's a work in progress too.

In my case, I'm on such a brand-new journey that planning becomes more interesting! Everything for me is new, including feeling honored as a co-author in this book series! I would have never guessed that this was in my future in a million years, and here I am, writing these chapters!

It's exhilarating and unexpected, as I said! You can't always plan on what's coming because we truly don't know, but when it does, be ready to jump on it, and don't procrastinate! You can be impulsive and still plan things out to get them accomplished. Take a pause. If you miss a deadline, just move it a bit! You'll get it done. Be patient with yourself, especially if you are going through an emotional situation, as I recently have. Life happens, and it's okay, take a step back, breathe, and keep going! Meditation can help regroup focus.

It's so easy for me to use my husband's recent passing to explain why I cannot do something! But instead, my reality is that I will do it for him and make him proud and honor him.

Don't ever take things for granted on your life's path and journey. You WILL get a wake-up call!

One other piece of advice is, "Wake up and SMELL THE ROSES on your way to success."

BONNIE LIERSE

About Bonnie Lierse: Bonnie Zaruches Lierse is extremely artistic and creative, with an entrepreneurial bent. Besides that, she is a seasoned agent with more than twenty years' experience in real estate in the New York/Long Island area. She relocated to Northern Virginia in 2012 and continued her real estate career there.

Another passion is creating leaders by working in business leadership development with Leadership Team Development (LTD), marketing products supplied by Amway. She was also a member of The Screen Cartoonist Guild of Motion Pictures for many years. Also, she did freelance for Sesame Street in New York City. In addition, she was a District Director for an interior accessory design company, as her own business.

Bonnie is blessed with five beautiful grandchildren and is very close with her children and family, some of whom are also in Virginia. Her missions, are leadership, mentorship, paying it forward, and changing lives one at a time. Her motto is "You be the difference!"

Author's Website: *www.amway.com/myshop/SplashFXEnterprises*
Book Series Website & Author's Bio: *www.The13StepstoRiches.com*

Brian Schulman

A PLAN ONLY WORKS IF YOU PROCEED WITH INTEGRITY

How did you go about bringing a new fraternity to a college campus that has a rich Greek history, strong Fraternal history, and a currently thriving Greek community?

Organized planning.

In the fall of 1991, four men had a vision. They decided to found a new chapter of the well- established national fraternity, Phi Kappa Theta. By Spring 1995, the 33 founding fathers grew to 74 members.

The End.

Not exactly.

So let's go back. These four men could only take it so far in the time they had. So they began a process, and, by using organized planning, my fellow founding charter members and I were able to see that vision to completion. We made their vision a reality. It came to life with us and continues to grow to this day.

We wanted to create something different. We wanted to be part of building something that would outlast our time at San Diego State University. That would leave a legacy. We wanted to have an impact for years to come.

We believed in the idea of building something with a strong heritage and creating history. Lifelong experiences that would shape who we were and the men we would become.

This would never have come to fruition without organized planning.

We had to get organized to be colonized in order to be recognized by the San Diego State University Interfraternity Council as a university-endorsed organization.

I joined the efforts in 1994, and in 1996 I became the charter organization's President. We took every step toward being recognized and accepted as part of the greater Greek community. We were different. Unique. But that did not mean that we did not want to be part of the already existing Greek family at San Diego State University. Instead, our mission was to add value while lifting up the Greek community and the university community at large. In doing so, we would have an impact and inspire others to follow suit. Being part of the growth of the Greek system, the commitment to brotherhood and leadership was an honor we were willing to work for. Ultimately, we wanted to help change the face and the 'stereotype' of Greek life and the Greek system.

Now, to grow from some guys hanging out to becoming a part of a long-established national organization took Organized Planning. There were clearly defined steps that needed to be taken and goals that had to be reached to continue moving forward.

There needed to be a commitment to a common goal and the essentials of Organized Planning. It called for unwavering courage and the willingness to assume full responsibility.

We were going against an already established tradition of which fraternities were historically on the row at San Diego State University. We had to work in a way that was mindful of the value these organizations held and be careful not to offend or disrespect them in our exuberance and excitement. We knew they were valuable partners with whom we wanted to be 'brothers.' Additionally, we would not be successful without their support and collaboration.

It meant finding a group of like-minded and like valued men who saw what we were trying to create, believed in what we were doing, and then asking them to commit to something with no guaranteed outcome, knowing, if we were not successful, it was on us as the founding members. No matter what, we were all committed that we would not move forward with anything that did not align with our integrity and values.

We were responsible not only for the successes but for what would inevitably 'go wrong'; as we know, no goal is achieved without a setback or two. We shouldered the full responsibility to, and for, the young men who trusted and "shared" our vision. Who believed in the dream and invested themselves? In addition, we were responsible for ourselves, remaining steadfast to the original goal of giving and expecting nothing thereof. To remain unwavering in the face of adversity and failure and not compromise or try and cut corners in the process, even if it seemed easier and faster. Giving up was not an option. The plan was there for a reason. It ensured success IF we stuck to it.

We made a commitment to maintaining and upholding the standards and legacy of brothers around the world, who, since 1889, have been holding the torch before us. Men such as President John F. Kennedy, Gene Kelly, Paul Allen, Cofounder of Microsoft and owner of the Seattle Seahawks & Portland Trail Blazers, Paul Galvin, Founder of Motorola, Paul Allaire, President Chairman and CEO of Xerox, Bob Hope…among others.

The process of creating anything requires self-control. Starting something new is exhilarating, but you must constantly check your intentions, your ego and avoid arrogance and hubris. When you're in 'creator mode,' it is easy to feel invincible and unstoppable. But, the truth is, you will not get far unless you have the self-control to avoid the pitfalls of ego and are willing to accept help from others and remain humble.

The best thought-out plan is destined to fail if those involved are not in the habit of doing more than paid for. There is truth to the phrase 'a labor of love,' especially when the trail you are blazing is not the path of least resistance, offers no guarantee for a successful outcome, and will 'peak' well after putting the work in.

It is the essential 'human aspect' of the plan. Without sympathy and understanding, the ability to make people feel seen, heard, and valued, you will never be able to build a solid foundation on which to reach your goal. First, you have to show people love if you want them to fall in love with the vision, the mission, and the universal guiding principles behind what you are creating. In the early days, this meant giving all a voice in the process and future. For us, it was a commitment to listen to all and create an organization that considered everyone a potential member. A house where people who felt marginalized and believed the system could do better would be totally accepted AND wanted to be a part of building that legacy. We were building an organization that would serve as an example to the fraternity and all campus organizations.

Building and teaching the power of collaboration within our own organization, the San Diego State University Greek system, and the international fraternity community wasn't enough. It was our responsibility to give others the opportunity to experience the power of collaborating and building relationships with other on-, and off-campus organizations, charities, and clubs to create an environment that respected and included all.

After looking at a number of national fraternities, those four men chose Phi Kappa Theta. On Feb 12, 1992, the first official meeting of the San Diego State University affiliate group of Phi Kappa Theta was then held.

The first year was very tough. They held weekly meetings on Thursday nights. It was more like a club than a fraternity. Their numbers varied between six and 12 in that year. In the Fall of 1993, with the help of the National office sending consultants, the fraternity focused on colonization. As a result of the newly elected executive board, of which I was a member, the organization grew from six to 33 members, making it one of the fastest-growing Greek organizations on campus.

To be different, break the mold and be leaders takes courage, commitment, humility, and, above all, Organized Planning.

BRIAN SCHULMAN

About Brian Schulman: A 5X #1 Best-Selling Author and internationally known Keynote Speaker, Brian Schulman is known as the Godfather, and Pioneer, of LinkedIn Video and one of the world's premier live streaming & video marketing experts whose insights have been featured on NASDAQ, ROKU and a #1 Best-selling live-streaming book.

With 20+ years of proven Digital Marketing experience strategizing with Fortune 500 brands across the globe, Brian founded & is the CEO of Voice Your Vibe, which brings his wealth of knowledge as an advisor and mentor to Founders & C-Suite Executives by providing workshops and 1-on-1 Mastery Coaching on how to voice their vibe, attract their tribe, and tell a story that people will fall in love with through the power and impact of live & pre-recorded video.

Named "2020 Best LIVE Festive Show of The Year" at the IBM TV Awards, his global award- winning weekly LIVE shows #ShoutOutSaturday & #WhatsGoodWednesday have been featured in Forbes, Thrive Global, Yahoo Finance, an Amazon best-selling book, and syndicated on a Smart TV Network. Among his many awards and honors, Brian has been named a 'LinkedIn Top Voice,' 'LinkedIn Video Creator Of The Year,' one of the 'Top 50 Most Impactful People of LinkedIn' out of 800 million people for three consecutive years and a 'LinkedIn Global Leader of The Year' for two consecutive years.

Beyond all the achievements and accolades, Brian is most proud of his two children and the connections and relationships he's made along the way.

Author's Website: *www.VoiceYourVibe.com*
Book Series Website & Author's Bio: *www.The13StepstoRiches.com*

Candace Rose

PLAN TO SUCCEED

As a self-titled organization specialist, I love this topic. Because even with the best intentions, a failure to plan is a plan to fail. I can't wait to see what Mel Mason says on this topic. She's Amazing.

We recently moved 1,200 miles to Texas. And as the final date quickly approached, I realized that burnout was imminent unless I had a plan. Luckily, that plan had been one of the first things I worked on when moving came up as a viable option.

And that plan involved playing and spending time with the people I love, just as much as it included hard work. And the work was HARD. But we had the promise of fun intertwined.

Sticking to that plan, knowing that we had scheduled breaks, got me through.

Knowing in advance what our limits on time and space were, was critical. And it meant that when we left, we were able to look to the future vs. hang on to the past.

Sometimes, organized planning includes NOT accounting for every step. For example, we knew we wanted to make it in three days. But planning extra time just in case we couldn't was a relief.

That's again where organized planning saved us. We made sure to budget for extra time and resources.

It gave us, once again, enjoyment in the task vs. tedium.

In my professional work, I charge a rate that people will not pay for me to waste.

This means that I'd better go into the job with a plan that makes the most efficient use of their money for my time.

They often have a budget as well. Nothing feels worse in a professional/ client relationship than leaving a job unfinished due to a lack of planning and not being prepared to finish inside that agreed budget because of it.

I often remind my children that "failure to plan on (their) part does not constitute an emergency on mine."

When we decided back in November to sell our house in Utah and relocate to Texas, our 19-year- old decided she did not want to come with us.

Had she failed to plan and waited until we were pulling away to come up with alternate living and transportation arrangements, she may have found herself reluctantly moving with us or without the security of a new arrangement there.

Our 17-year-old also wants to stay in Utah. However, she has yet to come up with a plan. So we are still going back and forth on what we're going to do. It is a much more stressful situation than the 19-year-old has—all due to the lack of an organized plan.

I couldn't imagine what we would be missing out on if we had not taken the time to organize our move. It was stressful and chaotic. But the knowledge that we had a plan and the ability to implement it saved us. We love our new adventure. We love fun. Make sure you allow for enjoyment whenever you make a plan. You'll be glad you did!

A few months prior to our move, I arranged to trade home organization for a course I was interested in. Unfortunately, the other party in the arrangement found themselves moving at the same time we were. This put me in the position of packing and organizing two households at once. I found myself running out of time. But I am a woman of my word. I was able, through careful planning, to arrange for someone to help us both. And neither of us had to go without when I just couldn't be in two places at once.

Have you ever seen the example of filling a jar with several large and small items? If you fill the jar with the little things first, there's no room left for the big things. But if you take the time to organize them and put the big ones in first, you can fit the smaller ones into the extra spaces.

May you always plan to succeed by successfully planning.

CANDACE ROSE

About Candace and David Rose: Candace Rose, is a #1 Best-Selling Author in the book series, The 13 Steps to Riches. Candace and her husband David (co-author to Candace in volumes 1-5) grew up together and currently live in Alvarado, Texas with their Six Children, three Chickens, two Dogs, four Cats and a rabbit. They both are veterans of the US Army. Her husband, David, served as a mechanic and Candace as a Legal NCO. David is currently a Product Release Specialist, delivering Liquid Oxygen and Nitrogen to various manufacturing plants and hospitals throughout Utah, Colorado, Idaho and Nevada. Candace is the owner of Changing Your Box Organization. Where she specializes in helping people organize their space, both physically and mentally—with the ultimate goal to help you change your box and find more joy in your life. Both Candace and David are proud members of the elite Champion Circle Networking Association in Salt Lake City, UT, founded by one of our co-authors of The 13 Steps To Riches book series, Jon Kovach Jr.

Author's Website: *www.ChangeYourBox.com*

Book Series Website & Author's Bio: *www.The13StepstoRiches.com*

Corey Poirier

BIO PLANNING 101

In considering the approach I would take for this chapter, there were so many options considering that the organized planning chapter includes so many elements of Hill's teachings – from definiteness of purpose to The Mastermind to the habit of doing more than paid for.

These elements of his teachings alone, and my approach to them, changed my life forever and for the better.

Still, I wanted to take an approach that I don't think everyone has in the past in relation to summarizing this powerful chapter in this powerful book.

And so, I wanted to talk about building your bio. Specifically, I want to talk about your business bio.

In this chapter, Hill focuses on how you can make yourself employable or have people desire to work with you specifically.

His focus, being more so on gaining employment, reflects the era. There certainly weren't as many 'captains of industry' or 'solopreneurs' in the 1930s as there are today.

In that time, having a powerful bio (or resume) certainly puts you in a better position for gainful employment.

Today, when so many people are jumping into the entrepreneurial waters, I wanted to focus on the business bio, as I believe if you are an entrepreneur who knows how to create and how to position a business bio correctly, it can lead to more clients, more credibility, more media, more exposure, better leverage and so much more.

For instance, being a best-selling author positions you better than someone in your industry who isn't a best-selling author to secure more clients.

Ask almost anyone if they had to choose between a dentist who wrote a book on dentistry and one who hasn't, which one they would rather go to. In my experience, most would prefer the one who wrote the book on it.

Not only that, often that dentist has more media opportunities and, as a result, can often charge more and has more clients than the competing dentist with no book.

So, fellow business owner, have you authored a book yet? If not, when will you?

Even if it's a compilation book, like this one you're reading, where you write a chapter, if it becomes a best-selling book, you are now a co-author of a best-selling book—and how great does that look on your bio, website, on social media and email signature?

Even if you aren't an entrepreneur, writing a book on your focus area will help you stand out from the crowd.

I used a book as an example, but it could be a TEDx Talk, speaking at a prestigious, writing for a magazine like *Forbes or Entrepreneur*, or appearing on a top radio show, tv show, or podcast.

Each time you add one of these to your business bio, which could even include media appearances on newer podcasts, you increase your value in the eyes of potential and future clients, even current clients, and how people view you and your expertise in general.

It's why Academy Award Winning Actors get paid more than their counterparts. People typically watch a movie, whether right or wrong, quicker when they see it has an Academy Award-winning actor in it, so movie studios pay more to have said actor in their movie.

It's also why Hall of Fame Wrestlers or Boxers get paid more to appear at events.

It's why TEDx speakers get paid more to speak than non-TEDx speakers or why celebrity speakers get paid more than non-celebrity speakers.

So again, the question is: Have you started building a business bio you can leverage and position?

A strong business bio will make you more indispensable, and believe it or not; people will listen closely to what you say, thus allowing you to have a greater impact.

So back to the question, have you authored a book yet?

Now again, you can insert landing a TEDx Talk or writing for a major magazine or whatever you prefer in place of authoring a book, but hopefully, you get the idea.

I simply want you to know how important it is to your business to build a business bio that can catapult you to a higher level.

So the first order of business is to take the steps needed to secure that achievement that elevates your business bio in the first place. Whether it means media reach-outs or reaching out to those who compile compilation books, or whichever achievement you choose to focus on, action is where it all begins.

The second order of business is to know how and where to leverage it.

For instance, every time you approach the media, make sure this new achievement is front and center for them to see.

This means it needs to be in the actual bio you submit when considering opportunities. It also should be in places I mentioned above, like your email signature.

If you do a lot of emailing, I actually believe your email signature is the best piece of unused real estate available to you.

So many people have nothing or very underwhelming things in their email signature, yet it's one of the things most people read first (after your email message) when you email them for the first time, AND it costs you nothing.

You should also have that new bio achievement somewhere on your website as well.

Social Media is also a place where it needs to be. I mean, how many people Google or check you out on LinkedIn or similar social platforms when deciding whether or not to do business with you.

Being a best-selling author or similar could be the one thing that moves them over the edge of deciding to work with you.

Not having that achievement, whichever one it is, or not including it in these places could be the difference between a media personality deciding to bring you onto their show, a client deciding to hire you, or even a future employer deciding to reach out about an opening in their company. Ultimately, your impact could be diminished simply because the achievement didn't happen or was left out.

So when we talk about organized planning, even though the bio may not be the main thing people talk about after reading the chapter, I believe the importance of having a powerful bio (or resume) can never be overstated.

I hope you'll decide to join me in creating a bio that you, and your future clients or colleagues, can be proud of.

Step 1: Take action on securing the achievement, and Step 2: Leverage that achievement everywhere possible.

It's just two 'simple' steps, but none of it happens until you take action. Until then, here's to your greater success.

COREY POIRIER

About Corey Poirier: Corey is a multiple-time TEDx Speaker. He is also the host of the top-rated Let's Do Influencing radio show, founder of The Speaking Program, founder of bLU Talks, and has been featured in multiple television specials. He is also a Barnes & Noble, Amazon, Apple Books, and Kobo Bestselling Author and the co-author of the *Wall Street Journal* and *USA Today* bestseller, *Quitless.*

A columnist with *Entrepreneur* and *Forbes* magazine, he has been featured in/on various mediums and is one of the few leaders featured twice on the popular *Entrepreneur on Fire* show.

Also appearing on the popular Evan Carmichael YouTube Channel, he is a New Media Summit Icon of Influence, was recently listed as the # 5 Influencer in Entrepreneurship by Thinkers 360, and listed on the 2021 Brainz CREA Global Awards as an honoree. He is an Entrepreneur of the Year Nominee, Champion Award (Business from The Heart) nominee, and to demonstrate his versatility, a Rock Recording of the Year Nominee who has performed stand-up comedy more than 700 times, including an appearance at the famed Second City..

Author's Website: *www.TheInfluencerVault.com*
Book Series Website & Author's Bio: *www.The13StepstoRiches.com*

Deb Scott

THE CRYSTALLIZATION OF DESIRE INTO ACTION

This sixth step toward riches takes what we learned about Desire into Imagination and translates these keys from the abstract into the concrete. We need the first two keys to get to this critical key called Action.

Hill describes the formation of these practical steps broken down within the construct of:

A. Ally yourself with a group of similar-minded people: a mastermind.
B. Be specific om the advantages and benefits of the mastermind to each individual involved in the mastermind.
C. Arrange to meet at least twice a week.
D. Commit to principles of the mastermind, keeping Harmony with all members.

The members' experience and their different abilities and imagination processes will help others gain success. Plans must be workable, and you must be persistent. You must have a faultless detailed plan to execute.

As we have learned on our journey together, mindset makes all the difference. Consider famous people you admire who have achieved the success you want, such as Thomas Edison. He is a great success in the eyes of history. Yet he "failed ten thousand times before perfecting the incandescent electric light bulb."

The key to anyone successful you can think of is that they reframed defeats into success and remained persistent in their ultimate imagined goal, which they desired to accomplish with all their mind, body, and spirit. "No man is ever whipped until he quits in his own mind." You must accept in advance that you WILL have temporary defeats and believe they are only temporary and keep going.

When I began real estate, I could not believe all the legality involved or how I would ever complete a successful transaction. I honestly still believe cardiac surgery sales in Boston were easier than doing real estate in Florida. As frustrated as I was with real estate, I imagined and desired to be a success because I never do anything without a desire to be the best at my attempt at whatever I decide to pursue. Did I quit? Did I let other people's values defeat my desire? Did I give up on believing in myself? No. I switched companies to a culture more aligned with my moral compass and goals and learned in a weekly mastermind group from one of this company's best. What did this accomplish for me? I won ICON for 2021, my third year in real estate, one of the highest sales awards in the United States for my company EXP Realty.

Did I want to give up? Yes. Did I have days I doubted my ability to accomplish my goal? Yes. Did I even shed tears of frustration and doubt? Yes. However, did I let those emotions stop me from following my plan for success? No.

You must accept that there will be setbacks and disappointments on any journey and incorporate those into your plan of success. 75% is the new 100% because there is no 100% in life in anything.

You have protected yourself from premeditated resentments when you adjust your expectations and give up five minutes before the miracle.

No student is great than his teacher. Hill goes into great detail about what determines a great leader. Review this list and make sure the leader you have selected as your teacher and mentor exhibits these qualities.

1. Unwavering Courage
2. Self-Control
3. A keen sense of Justice
4. Definiteness of decision
5. Definiteness of Decision
6. The habit of doing more than paid for
7. A pleasing personality
8. Sympathy and Understanding
9. Mastery of Detail
10. Willingness to assume full Responsibility
11. Cooperation

You want a leader who leads by consent, not by force. That would be a dictator. Leaders are good leaders because followers decide of their own free will. They are authentic winners with something of value, which they have proven to share with great results.

Equally as important is knowing what you don't want and whom to avoid. Hill also supplies a detailed list of 10 major causes of failure in leadership. Check this list against the leader or mentor you are deciding to work with before signing on with them.

1. Inability to organize details
2. Unwillingness to render humble service
3. The expectation of pay for what they know instead of what they do with what they know
4. Fear of Competition from Followers
5. Lack of Imagination
6. Selfishness
7. Intemperance
8. Disloyalty
9. Emphasis on the authority of leadership
10. Emphasis on title

Make sure you are free of these faults yourself as well.

If you are wondering what areas or fields will require this new type of new leadership, I would say all. Since COVID, social media, and morality, the world has changed so much. I believe we need a fresh start in any type of business of living or business of business.

For example, I believe real estate is not life or death like my experience in cardiac surgery sales, but I also believe it should be. Selling or buying a house is the biggest financial investment you will ever make for most people in their lives. This deserves attention to detail and a serious, educated professional, just like working with a surgeon in the operating room to ensure optimum results are achieved for the patient while his heart is beating.

One of my goals is to make real estate more professional, like cardiac surgery sales. A sense of urgency, honesty, education, service, follow-up, detail, communication, and going above and beyond what is required. I think this belief has contributed greatly to my quick success, but it is not without time and sacrifice. Personally, the nearly 50 five-star reviews and friends I have made along the way are equally as important to me in the sale as the actual closing day and monetary reward. Money alone is never a solid motivator; you must have the vision and desire using your imagination of a new outcome you want to accomplish to remain persistent through those inevitable emotional and financial ups and downs.

At the time of his writing his book, Hill describes some fields that will require new leaders: Politics, Banking, Industry, Religious Leaders, Law, Medicine, Education, and Journalism.

When Hill wrote his book, he did not have social media, which is now the #1 platform for marketing and communication. Therefore, it might not be a bad idea to go back to the basics and consider using some of the old fashion ways of marketing your services for success, such as Employment Bureaus, Advertising newspapers, trade journals, magazines, radio, Personal letters of Application, Application through Personal Acquaintances, Application in Person.

I have always found people buy from people they "Know, Like, and Trust." When you engage all five senses, you are more likely to accomplish this goal. So how do you activate all five senses most effectively? In-person, of course. The best tried and true method of success in my sales has always been through one-on-one conversation. You can't fake being real.

Hill also describes what should be included in your written brief. I would consider this a good marketing tool to gain business because your customer does not know what they do not know. Your customer does not know how much they need you and why you are different in a much better way for them to hire. You must humbly prove to them that you are the best.

1. Education
2. Experience
3. References from former employers and teachers. Prominent people
4. Photograph of Self
5. Apply for a specific position and be precise
6. State your qualification
7. Offer to go to work on probation without pay
8. Knowledge of your prospective employers' business

"When the time comes to perform, the time to prepare has passed."
~ Olympic Medalist, Peter Vidmar

You must take the time to do your homework to create a precise plan to succeed. This is your map to your goal.

Hill describes how to get the exact position you desire. These include: Decide Exactly what kind of a job you want; Choose the company; Study your prospective employer; By analysis of yourself, your talent, and capabilities, figure out what you can offer; Forget about "a job"; Put on paper in full detail your plan and present it to the proper person with authority.

Suppose you want to create something or a position that has never been created before. You can use these similar steps. Begin with the end in mind. If I want to change how salespeople do sales, I must know how those results are accomplished. I must have a vehicle in place to reach my target audience and the training and value they can easily duplicate to accomplish the success I am promising to deliver if they follow the plan. This requires time and research, a survey of the current landscape of what people want, and my personal experience. If I want to create something that has never been created before, I must use all these steps we have learned throughout each chapter in Hill's book to get there.

I love how Hill describes the New "Golden Rule" will not be the old "Rule of Gold." I completely agree with this philosophy now more than ever. People are tired of being treated like a number, lacking personal respect or high customer service. It seems to me that social media has stunted our growth to respect people as dignified human beings who should be treated as if they are your only customer. People are starving for authenticity and accountability. I truly believe the new wave of winners in the world will conduct business with truth, accountability, authenticity, and a good sense of humor. They will be humble and care deeply that the success of the other is the success of themselves. The shift of entitlement is over. Hard work and the personal touch have never gone out of style.

In closing, Hill gives a great list of 28 questions to ask yourself for a successful personal inventory. I won't list them all here except for one. I believe this sums it all up in a nice, neat package. It's number 25 on his list but, in my opinion, the only one that matters.

Hill said, *"If I had been the purchaser of my own services for the year, would I be satisfied with my purchase?"*

In my opinion, you haven't truly sold anything until you get a repeat customer or a loyal customer who refers your name without even asking.

Would you buy from you?

DEB SCOTT

About Deb Scott: Deb Scott, BA, CPC, and Realtor was a high honors biology major at Regis College in Weston, Massachusetts, and spent over two decades as an award-winning cardio-thoracic sales specialist in the New England area. She is a best-selling author of *The Sky is Green & The Grass is Blue: Turning Your Upside Down World Right Side Up.* She is an award-winning podcaster of The Best People We Know Show. Following in her family's footsteps, she is a third generation Realtor in Venice, Florida. As a certified life coach, Deb speaks and teaches on how to turn bad situations into positive, successful results. As a top sales specialist, she enjoys teaching people "sales without selling," believing that integrity, good communication, and respect are the winning equation to all outstanding success and happiness in life.

Author's Website: *www.DebScott.com*
Book Series Website & Author's Bio: *www.The13StepstoRiches.com*

Dori Ray

TO BE OR NOT TO BE...
THAT IS THE QUESTION

When I sat down to write, so many things crossed my mind. As I revisited this section of Napoleon Hill's *Think and Grow Rich,* I thought it was to prepare to write my chapter. It had been a long time since I sat down and really read the section on Organized Planning. It turned out that it was a "date with destiny." While reading through the pages, I begin to receive a revelation that I know will turn my entire career and life around. For many years, in my profession of Network Marketing, I have heard people refer to this book as the foundation upon which their successful careers were built. I admired many people who, from stages, recommended that we read this book from cover to cover so that we can achieve the levels of success we dreamed of as aspiring budding entrepreneurs. They also mentioned that they would refer back to it at many points and stages in their career. It was said that this was one of the books that separated the men from the boys, the women from the girls, and the successful from the unsuccessful. It was apparent that there were some secrets and sound principles in this book that had the ability to turn one's business into a successful income-building machine!

Re-reading Hill's chapter on Organized Planning made me ask myself some very critical questions. I am at a point in my career where I have hit a lid. I am no longer experiencing the joy I had over the last 20-plus years as a Network Marketer, and I was beginning to question my journey. I felt as if I had wasted decades chasing rabbits that could never be caught. I realized that there was a hole in my bucket, and it needed to be plugged in immediately. I was experiencing a moment or short season of temporary defeat, and it was getting the best of me. I questioned how I could have gone this many years without taking inventory of my life and career! This chapter halted me in my tracks and made me address some very difficult questions. Questions that should have been asked and answered many years ago. Completing this inventory could've probably saved me a lot of pain and suffering and generated a lot of dollars and cents!

At the young age of 33 years old, 25 years ago, I was introduced to the industry of Network Marketing. I remember my father's words to me: "You have lost your mind!" He wondered how I could look at my four years of college, his huge investment, and my beautiful degree and decided to join one of "those things," as he called it. But something about "that thing" had touched me in my gut. It felt right, and I could not shake the feeling that I had "found home."

When I discovered Network Marketing, I was working as a pharmaceutical sales representative for a major company and was even making more money than my dad. I pretended to be happy but hated the job every day. Although this provided a healthy income, I was always feeling defeated, empty, and dissatisfied. I can still remember what the room looked like when I saw this industry for the first time. When I walked into the room that night, I learned something that I had never been taught in high school, college, or even in my home. What I heard in that room made sense, and I knew that day, at that moment, there was no going back. The icing on the cake was that everyone was hopeful, cheerful, and routing for everyone to win. That was very different from the moaning and complaints I heard every time I attended a meeting with my pharmaceutical teammates.

That night I decided that this was where I belonged. Don't get me wrong; I went back to work. I had no other option. I was a single mom with two young daughters. I had just purchased my new home. Going full-time was not an option, so I decided to start part-time and eventually make this my full-time occupation! I had a plan, and I was ready to execute it. The thought of joining a winning team was exciting to me! I had never heard people speak of success in this way. The thought of being part of a Mastermind team where everyone could get to the top awakened something in me that died at the age of 9, the end of my 3rd grade year in school. In pharmaceutical sales, it was always dog-eat-dog for the race to the number one spot that I pretended to want.

That night was the first time I decided to do something that set my soul on fire. I did something that I hadn't had the courage to do since I was nine years old. I was doing what I wanted and not what pleased my dad! I just could not deny the feeling I felt when I walked into that Amway meeting. It was magical! Network marketing felt like home. It was an instant attraction. The entrepreneur in me had been awakened. I began to dream again! For the first time, I was even willing to disappoint my father. That in itself was MAJOR. For a quick moment, I considered how disappointing my choice to do "one of those things" would be to my father. But the desire was stronger than the fear of not being accepted. I had no idea what I was getting into, but I followed my gut. I had to start part-time. I intended to work this thing part-time, but my ultimate goal was to stand on one of those stages and tell my story of how the network marketing profession led me to obtain all my dreams and goals. I was also excited about helping other people do the same and having fun the whole time. Everything about this industry was appealing to me!

Ironically, I did not make any money at Amway, but the experience of working in mastermind teams changed my life forever. It was here, in this profession, that I was first introduced to the whole concept of a mastermind team. Before network marketing, in Corporate America, the strategy was definitely every man for himself. The goal was to be number one and do whatever it took to get there. But in network marketing, I learned that teamwork actually made the dream work.

When I joined my 3rd real network marketing company, I began, after about four years of temporary defeat after defeat, the importance and major role of the mastermind team kicked into effect. This was the first time I became a six-figure earner and hit the industry's top 10% of earners. This team had all the qualities I was looking for, and I knew this was "The Big One." I loved how this mastermind team operated, and I was very clear on why we were experiencing major success. One thing we did, which was life-changing, was to meet every day at 5:30 am to set the tone of our day, set goals, and speak out affirmations and mantras. Our team was unstoppable. The company had never seen a team move with such precision. We were treated like royalty, and rightfully so! We were producing millions of dollars for the company.

Then something happened. I watched the team crumble as egos began to swell, bad relationships began to form, and trust was violated. I watched my income tumble at the same rate at which the mastermind team became polluted with the very things Mr. Hill told us to avoid. At my lowest point, I allowed temporary defeat to convince me to quit the profession I had come to love and go back into a "regular job." Needless to say, the dissatisfaction of being back to regular work was more than I could handle. I became sad and even had another episode of depression.

After some time, I had an opportunity to rejoin another team in Network Marketing with a different company. This team had all of the qualities of my first winning team. For the next five years, we modeled all of the qualities of the team in my first company, and I became a 6-figure earner once again in that company. Then, it seemed like the team that I was leading began to crumble out of nowhere. The huge mistake I made this time, and with the last team, if I'm totally honest, is that I was better at evaluating the faults of others than I was at evaluating myself. I did a lot of blaming and finger-pointing, which ultimately led to me experiencing my second big fall in the industry I loved. I also watched my income go backward week after week. Again, I decided it was them and not me and decided to leave the company.

Instead of a break in between, I immediately started with a new company, and the feeling was back. However, something was different. I had a burst of initial success and then quickly hit a wall. Instead of going back to work, I started to give my attention to lots of other things chasing that feeling I got from the industry over two decades ago that just was not returning. Nothing seemed to satisfy me or last long. I could not figure out why, once again, I was feeling empty and unfulfilled.

That brings me to today and back to my first thought as I sat down to listen to this chapter so that I could complete my assignment. I'm leading a team that is not winning on any level. (This is transparency at its highest level). I had forgotten, or let's say, was unwilling to admit, how important it was as a leader to take personal responsibility for my success or failure. More importantly, I needed to take responsibility for the success or failure of my team. From my years of work, I know that everything rises and falls on LEADERSHIP. I was trying to circumvent the learning and growing process and just "get to the money!" Finally, I found the answer to questions that have been in my head and heart for years. I was reminded that I had control over my wins and losses. I was also reminded that my role on the mastermind team was to honor all of the requirements.

Instead, I have to admit that I had begun to violate not one but many of these mandates necessary for success. I felt amazing learning, for the umpteenth time, that this "Temporary Defeat" had to be acknowledged and that I must get busy working on myself. I needed a tune-up. That was the only thing that would repair the "holes in my bucket." Now that I've accepted my role in the demise of my dream, I know I have the power to change and fix those things that are causing problems and hindering my success and the success of the team. This time I'm not going to quit the profession that has given me the ability to meet amazing people. It has given me the time, freedom to care for my sick father, and the opportunity to explore other goals and make them a reality. And, when working properly, had paid me quite nicely!

As I close out this chapter, I recommend that if you are at a place in your life or career where you're feeling unfulfilled and unsuccessful, do a PERSONAL inventory. Correct the parts of you that are no longer lining up with your goals, accept the temporary defeat as a great lesson and become the person you desire to attract and serve. I was reminded that some tools, like *Think and Grow Rich,* should be in your daily toolbox and reached for whenever you feel broken and off track.

DORI RAY

About Dori Ray: Dori "On Purpose" Ray is a native Philadelphian. As a businesswoman, her mission is to help people transform their minds, bodies, and bank accounts!

Dori was educated in the Philadelphia Public School System. She graduated from the Philadelphia High School for Girls in 1982 and Howard University School of Business in 1986 with a BBA in Marketing. Dori is a member of Delta Sigma Pi Business Fraternity and Delta Sigma Theta Sorority, Inc.

Dori leads teams around the world. She is a sought-after Speaker and Trainer within her industry and beyond. She is an experienced Re-Entry Coach as she has helped hundreds of Returning Citizens get back on track after incarceration.

Having suffered from depression for 20 years, she always reaches back to share her story and help break the cycle of silence. Her audience loves her authenticity!

Book Dori for speaking engagements www.linktr.ee/dorionpurpose

Author's Website: *www.linktr.ee/DoriOnPurpose*
Book Series Website & Author's Bio: *www.The13StepstoRiches.com*

Elaine Sugimura

FAILURE CREATES MASTERY

As I reflect on my fashion career as a CEO, I now recognize what worked and what did not! How many times did it take me to shift into knowing what was in the GAP as the CEO of a given business? As I ask these questions to myself now, I can see where I missed pivoting in a few of my past management experiences. By anyone's standards, I achieved the pinnacle of success. Yet, I know there was more that could have been accomplished to exceed the standards set for myself and the businesses I managed and led as a Senior Executive.

Without discounting all that was achieved, I can remember a specific moment when I was challenged to create a business from a start-up position. It required keen insight into Napoleon Hill's Leadership Attributes. Specifically, Item #5 – Definiteness of Plans. One of the top things that one must do to succeed or maximize their results is to have a solid, organized plan. This is one thing that the majority of individuals and businesses fail to create and implement effectively. Hill says this about the definiteness of plans, "The successful leader must plan his work and work his plan. A leader who moves by guesswork without definite practical plans is comparable to a ship without a rudder. Sooner or later, he will land on the rocks."

If you fail to plan, your results will be exactly that – failure! Also, failing to work the plan will be your next challenge. We often develop plans that support the initial purpose and vision of a business. This is valuable, but the maximum value comes to fruition after you have worked with the plan from the strategy stage to driving it to its completion.

That moment I spoke to earlier was when I was hired as the CEO of Havaianas USA. The vision and mission for the US business were clear. Launch the brand by creating top-of-mind awareness in department and specialty stores nationwide. The budget was 10M dollars to set the entire business up in New York City, and the GO LIVE date was to be within six months. It was a daunting project, to say the least, especially when there was no "home" nor team members in place when I was hired. I was challenged to create an organized plan that included the following:

Step One: Vision - What is the End Goal?
Step Two: Current - Where are you right NOW?
Step Three: Agreement - Where is the GAP?
Step Four: Strategy/Plan - How to close the GAP?
Step Five: Execution - Organized Plan

By creating the vision of what we wanted to accomplish for the brand, we created a strategy that allowed us to meet the end goal! Having established the result we were looking for allowed us to move from each quadrant seamlessly. We hired the appropriate partners to execute the areas we could not execute on our own. Time was of the essence, and remember, we had zero staff nor office space, so as we built each section of the organized plan and relied on partners to share their space and team. They were connected to the project from the start and were key to the overall success. But, during the build process, we constantly had to pivot from the original plans as to when actual costs and execution began; key areas needed to be adjusted.

Of course, we continued to be challenged along the way, and certain parts of the organized plan did not work. Hill stated that a plan is not a guarantee for success, saying, "Temporary defeat should mean only one thing, the certain knowledge that there is something wrong with your plan." In other words, keep reworking the plan - if it fails, try again; if it fails again, try again. The moral of this story is to be persistent in what you are creating, as you cannot reap the rewards unless you keep adjusting what is not working. This included every part of the organized plan. If the people you hired have not met expectations, adjust. If a partner you have relied on to complete parts of the strategy fails to meet their end of the deal, adjust. Finally, if it is YOU, what can you do to shift to ensure the project's success? We must constantly challenge ourselves to see, hear and pivot when the plan is not moving forward as planned.

Measuring one's progress means knowing that you are moving in the right direction. If it feels off, shift. Waiting to the end to assess what is working and what is not working may be too late. Be connected and in relationship to your plan, at its core, and remember it is just that, a plan. It is a forecast of what you believe can be done. Our plans are full of assumptions. We know that assumptions may be wrong, and what if they are wrong? This is what we call RISK!

When we speak about risk, we get to ask ourselves, "What choices are available to us?" Usually, we land at being proactive to the risk as we plan or reactive when the actual result presents itself. Typically, it always feels right to be proactive so that we mitigate any risk from the start. To have an organized plan, the team must review the following questions as they plan for risk:

Question One: What assumptions are there?
Question Two: If the assumption is incorrect,
                what new risk is presented in the plan?
Question Three: Is it likely the risk will occur?
Question Four: What impact does the risk have on the overall plan?
Question Five: How can you avoid the risk or minimize the impact?

Of course, none of us has a crystal ball, so the key is to present all possible risks to your plan to better prepare for what may happen and shift, as needed, to stay on course.

So with these tools in place, I built a team of six All-Star players. Each had a unique talent to bring to the table, and we began executing the organized plan. Marketing a brand that was well known in Brazil did not necessarily translate to selling $18.00 to $22.00 fashion flip-flops. We spent a great deal of time with masterful marketing initiatives to create the buzz in the market. From VIP events and trade shows to our national marketing campaigns, we created the necessary buzz to build the brand from the ground up. What often gets discounted is the amount of "back office" work required to ensure 100% success. We were flexible and often pivoted to ensure the end result would be the retailers chasing us vs. us chasing them. We created a commodity they desired, and we filled a gap on the retail floor that was not occupied at that time. We continued to build the brand by introducing new models and price points, always creating what was absent in the market. We continued to re-evaluate the cyclical plan and applied it to each area of the business structure. Through key relationships and partnerships, each step of the organized planning process worked! The launch was a success! The business grew from zero to multi-millions of dollars over two years. The lesson here is that this result would never have happened without the organized plan. To fail and try again was our mantra. We knew that there was no other option than pivot whenever we encountered a roadblock. It made the final outcome and success that much sweeter.

I also want to share that the key to a successfully organized plan is to be nimble and flexible. It was critically important that we were not attached to how the outcome and success had to look like. To achieve this level of success requires leadership in its truest form. The leader must possess the following leadership qualities: power, courage, commitment, generosity, empathy, contribution, urgency, rigor, responsibility, enrollment, communication, and teamwork. Without these characteristics, a leader will run into navigating a rudderless ship. So the moral of this story is to accept failure as a means to master your plan/strategy. Without failure, one does not learn how to get back up and create what, ultimately, is a WIN/WIN for everyone involved.

I want to leave you with one last thought. Failure creates Mastery! Let that soak in, and think of this when you fail on your next project or assignment. Keep challenging yourself to figure out what is in the GAP, the risks, and what assumptions you can make to ensure you have covered every possible scenario. What is waiting on the other side, you ask? The answer is pure success if you are willing to get back up each and every time you fall.

ELAINE SUGIMURA

About Elaine R. Sugimura: Elaine is an accomplished CEO turned Business Consultant / Life Strategist who has a passion to create Leaders amongst Leaders. With over 35+ years in the fashion and food and beverage industry, she has a passion to not only lead but support those who are seeking to reinvent who they are no matter where they are in life. She is a two-time breast cancer survivor and she knows a thing or two about surviving to thriving. Fun fact: she is an adrenaline junkie—the higher, the faster, the better. Her love for adventure has led her to travel to many parts of the world by plane, train and automobile. She and her husband, Hiro, share their home in Northern California. They have raised two extraordinary sons, Bryce and Cole and have added two beautiful daughters-in-law, Erica and Giselle to their growing family. Her legacy is to share what is possible when we open ourselves up to the issues that hold us back. Her life's mission is to move those who are just surviving into Thrivers!

Author's Website: *www.ElaineRSugimura.com*
Book Series Website & Author's Bio: *www.The13StepstoRiches.com*

Elizabeth Anne Walker

HOW TO BE A LEADER

Benjamin Franklin said, "If you fail to plan, you are planning to fail."

Many people believe that planning is the key to action, and in the past, it possibly was. However, the invention of smartphones and computers has meant that calendars and lists are readily available for most people. You may think that this would lead to more organization. Unfortunately, I believe it has led to less. The constant bombardment of our psyche with "do this do that," "there's an alarm for this, there's an alarm for that," "you must this, you must that," has led to a mental overload and physical stress that paralyzes the majority.

Deadlines, key performance indicators (KPIs), expectations, competitiveness, and social isolation at the hands of work hours have led to a less committed society than in previous generations. Worse still, corporate organized masterminds and thinktanks at the lower levels more often breed contempt than productivity as people strive to lead the group instead of leading themselves. As opposed to individual desire for money, societal distaste for money has led to a conflict for many that is overwhelmingly difficult to resolve. I believe this has led to, particularly in Australia, an overall weak society. So, what can we do about it?

Surrounding yourself with like-minded people, that is, people who have the same values, drive, and level of principled action, is the key to success.

Napoleon Hill said to create a mastermind, and I wonder if you've ever done this? I have done it several times, and finally, I feel as though I have an effective mastermind at this point in my life. That wasn't always the case.

"You are the average of the five people you spend the most time with."
~ Jim Rohn

My mom used to say if you sleep with the dogs, you'll get fleas. And at the time she said it, I loved my dogs and actually thought she was talking about sleeping with my dogs. As I grew, I watched this saying become more and more true. And whenever I spent time with "the dogs," I eventually "got fleas." I remember when I first started my business, everything was great. My husband and I ran it, and we got the idea to expand.

We entered into a partnership, and we thought that this would make our business grow and expand faster than ever. The couple that we partnered with were acquaintances of ours, and from what we'd seen of them, they appeared to have the same values as us. I was a workaholic, so I initially didn't notice the work that wasn't being done. Over time this small mastermind of four people started to crack. The harmony was lost. A true mastermind maintains harmony to the best of all its members' ability.

We ran a retreat together a few weeks before our first large event together, and thank goodness for that! Our business was built on supporting and lifting women who had been through significant abuse seeking healing. The women were offered a massage during the retreat by one of our business partners. Tragically one of the women had the experience of being touched inappropriately. After we had assisted her in having closure and leaving the retreat with ongoing counseling, we approached our business partners about it. The discussion felt like an accusation, and it became apparent that our partners could only deal with conflict through the emotion of anger. Something that we had never done. We realized it was time to go it alone again. We splintered the partnership and split the next day.

Within 24 hours of this split, an incredible group of people gathered around me to support me in running our first big event. This group of people became our first true mastermind. This mastermind consisted of friends and acquaintances who happened to be in business in very different fields from ours, yet their skills and advice were transferable. Better still, our skills and advice were also transferable to them. The mastermind consisted of a marketing merchandiser, a mobile telephone store operator, a supermarket owner, and a farmer. It was perfect, and I will forever remain grateful for this first mastermind. When planning a mastermind of your own, ensure you do it consciously and ensure it is a "win/win" for everyone in the group.

Now back to my rant at the beginning, planning is essential, and some plans don't go according to plan. This is feedback. There is no failure, only feedback. When I had my first son, I utilized a parenting book written in 1901. It worked for me. It was disciplined, it was principled, and it had old-fashioned values. In business, success occurs when the business owner and everyone in it is disciplined and principled and share the same values. Some people believe that leadership is for leaders, which is not true. Real leadership is the leadership of self, and when this is mastered, there is no need for a million alarm clocks, there is no need for KPIs, and there is no need for deadlines. Why? Because a leader will hold themselves accountable and achieve the tasks to the highest standard within the shortest appropriate timeframe.

Napoleon Hill identified two types of leadership: leadership by consent and leadership by force. Some of the most successful entrepreneurial companies encourage leadership by consent. This doesn't mean that the workers consent to be led by another. Instead, this means that everyone can be a leader of themselves, thus producing far more effective work product.

You may be asking what leadership has to do with planning? Planning becomes part of a daily routine, and results follow when one leads themselves. Napoleon Hill, in his book, *Think and Grow Rich*, identified 11 major attributes of leadership. I have decided to rework them slightly for the modern world as follows:

1. Self-Confidence - knowing oneself is the key. If you know yourself and are confident in who you are, others will choose to support you as they can gain certainty from you
2. Discipline - your ability to be disciplined with your thoughts, words, and actions will create great results and allow others to only speak highly of you
3. Be principled - upholding your principles, values, and morals allows you to make decisions swiftly and move on. This creates speed of achievement
4. Have a clear outcome- focusing on the outcome rather than the journey allows for more creative ways of achieving a goal. This gives the people around you the flexibility to work in the best way for them and still move forward towards the goal
5. Highly value yourself and others - create an environment where people are handsomely rewarded based on merit. Gone are the days of paying low commissions; pay yourself and your team what you deserve and what will keep you committed to the mission
6. Go above and beyond - always exceeding expectations will ensure the longevity of your business
7. Be Happy - happiness is an emotion many people are seeking in today's world. If you are happy, it allows others to be happy
8. Have Compassion - be in the community sharing passion. This allows everyone to grow together
9. Details and Big Picture - a great leader can share the big picture as well as hold all the tiny pieces of detail at the same time
10. Collaborate based on a mission - when you meet people with a similar mission to yours, create collaborations that support both of you individually as well as the greater mission

11. Accept Responsibility - whatever happens in your business falls on you as the leader. Accepting responsibility minimizes blame culture and creates better results.

So, what is my real point in this chapter? If you choose to lead yourself, then all forced methods of leadership like deadlines and KPIs become moot. Leading yourself will allow you to achieve far more than you ever thought was possible. Learning and implementing the above 11 principles is a life's work. Every time you up-level the principals, there is a new way of fulfilling them. So ask yourself, am I happy with the way that I am leading myself? Am I willing to take responsibility? Can I choose to be happy? And as you start to lead yourself, notice what happens around you. Notice how others change and grow. Notice that your willingness to plan yourself, take action yourself, and lead yourself rubs off on others, and everyone around you gets to elevate. Sure, there will be the occasional person who drops off; let them go. But, it may be the very thing that allows them to start leading themselves.

Start now! Who are the five people you want to spend time with? Who is in the mastermind you choose to create? Who are the dogs, and how can you get rid of the fleas? What will you plan so as to succeed in life?

ELIZABETH WALKER

About Elizabeth Walker: Elizabeth is Australia's leading Female Integrated NLP Trainer, an international speaker with Real Success, and the host of Success Resources' (Australia's largest and most successful events promoter, including speakers such as Tony Robbins and Sir Richard Branson) inaugural Australian Women's Program "The Seed." Elizabeth has guided many people to achieve complete personal breakthroughs and phenomenal personal and business growth. With over 25 years of experience transforming the lives of hundreds of thousands of people, Elizabeth's goal is to assist leaders to create the reality they choose to live, impacting millions on a global scale.

A thought leader who has worked alongside people like Gary Vaynerchuck, Kerwin Rae, Jeffery Slayter, and Kate Gray, Elizabeth has an outstanding method of delivering heart with business.

As a former lecturer in medicine at the University of Sydney and lecturer in nursing at Western Sydney University, Elizabeth was instrumental in the research and development of the stillbirth and neonatal death pathways, ensuring each family in Australia went home knowing what happened to their child, and felt understood, heard, and seen.

A former Australian Champion in Trampolining and Australian Dancesport, Elizabeth has always been passionate about the mindset and skills required to create the results you are seeking.

Author's website: *www.ElizabethAnneWalker.com*
Book Series Website & Author's Bio: *www.The13StepsToRiches.com*

Erin Ley

THREE CHEERS FOR VIOLETA

Napoleon Hill brilliantly states in his book, *Think and Grow Rich,* "You have learned that everything man creates or acquires, begins in the form of desire, that desire is taken in the first lap of its journey, from the abstract to the concrete, into the workshop of the imagination, where plans for its transition are created and organized."

I have experienced this principle, Organized Planning, personally and professionally, with great success. Regarding the cancer experience in 1991, I had the white-hot burning desire to heal my body. My imagination brought me to meditate on and visualize what exactly it was I needed to do. Then organized planning began to bring my desire to fruition. The sequence of events at that time was not a coincidence. The divine download began, and the steps I needed to take were laid out for me in such a beautifully organized way. The doctors and I worked together. I then organized my thoughts and wrote down my action steps, implementing my well-thought-out organized plan for my road to excellent health.

I have done the same professionally regarding Organized Planning. After a tumultuous divorce caused a financial conundrum, I had the white-hot burning desire to grow my business to six figures to start. I had been an Empowerment & Success Coach, Author, and Speaker for decades, yet I had to put all of that on hold for a few years to focus on my family and my transformation into the identity of a single mom. I was with my ex-husband for twenty-two years, so this adjustment needed to be nurtured.

As I walked through the transition and grew even stronger on the other side, I knew what I needed to do. I quieted my mind long enough to allow the organized planning to occur, knowing my white- hot-burning-desire was to provide the very best life I could for my three children and myself. My imagination was the playground for what was possible, the sky being not the limit but rather just the beginning. Then, organized planning began to take place. Divine organized planning and my own. I wrote down what Napoleon Hill refers to as a Mission Statement. It was a detailed, crystal- clear plan of what I needed to do to get me to six figures making a huge impact in the lives of others as and Empowerment & Success Coach, Author, and Speaker.

I knew my teams needed to develop both personally and professionally. One of the biggest and best investments in my personal team was when I decided to hire a cleaning lady. Violeta is what I call God-Given. She came at exactly the right time, four years ago, and is still with me to this day. She freed up my time to grow my business once again. She did that, but she also organized my home in such a beautiful way. Every week she cleans and organizes my home. She moves things around, shifting the energy in the home. Three cheers for Violeta! I love and appreciate her dearly!

Professionally, my business has grown exponentially with organized planning. I do not do things randomly like the expression says to throw spaghetti against the wall and see if it sticks. I'm methodical and intentional about how I grow my business. It's organized planning. My business and my team keep expanding. I've grown my business to six figures, and I have hired business and financial coaches to help me grow to seven figures. I hired an amazing assistant/tech genius/marketing master, a woman who helps with branding, graphic designers, appointment setters, content creators, branding photographer, a media company that I host my online streaming tv show through, and I've joined Erik Swanson's Habitude Warrior Mastermind. Napoleon Hill talks about how important a mastermind is when growing a business. I credit Erik's mastermind for the speed at which my company is growing, and I'm growing it with grace and ease.

If something I do along the way is not working, I change my plan and test new waters. In *Think and Grow Rich*, Napoleon Hill says, "Temporary defeat should mean only one thing, the certain knowledge that there is something wrong with your plan. Millions of men [and women] go through life in misery and poverty because they lack a sound plan through which to accumulate a fortune." If you have a plan that is not working, either personally or professionally, adjust the sails. Accept the temporary defeat instead of quitting altogether, resulting in self-imposed failure. Instead, move onward and upward with a new plan.

One of the most significant things we can do when growing our lives or our business is to make committed decisions. When we are indecisive or just interested in something without being committed, we will back down or back away at the first sign of a struggle or challenge. When we decide we are committed to it, we will make it happen come hell or high water. We will have inspired thoughts leading us to create an organized plan on how to take the inspired action. The committed decisions we make become steps on our pathway to success. In *Think and Grow Rich*, Napoleon Hill says, "Men who succeed reach decisions promptly and change them, if at all, very slowly. Men who fail reach decisions, if at all, very slowly and change them frequently and quickly. Indecision and procrastination are twin brothers. Where one is found, the other may usually be found. Also, kill off this pair before they completely 'hog-tie' you to the treadmill of failure."

When I interviewed Don Green on the Life On Track Summit, President & CEO of The Napoleon Hill Foundation, Don spoke eloquently and firmly about how destructive indecision and procrastination are and TV shows. When we sit in procrastination or put off making a committed decision, we end up doubting ourselves. Doubt is a dream crusher. When self-doubt creeps in, we usually end up in some form of fear. It could be regret, remorse, resentment, scarcity, anxiety, depression, anger, or any other form of fear. The fear always stems back to having not decided, making the firm decision that we will do something or not. The organized planning we need to lead us toward our desired outcome, our ultimate success, does not have room for indecision or procrastination. Success is built on making one decision after the next, making decisions quickly, and changing our minds infrequently, only after finding out a better decision can be made.

What opportunities do you have in front of you? What organized planning can you do to map out your road to success personally and professionally? You want to stay in your lane and keep your life and business on track. One of the greatest ways to do that is with organized planning. Quiet your mind and allow God and the Universe to gift you with inspired ideas. Use the new information you receive and the knowledge you already have to create your organized plan. Document it. There is an incredible power to putting pen to paper and writing down exactly what you want and the steps you need to take to get you there. This is something you will consistently build upon as you grow.

Decide you will no longer allow opportunities to pass you by. Be strategic in your approach to whatever you want to build and grow. Be intentional and mindful of your daily activity and decisions throughout your day. Do not quit if something is not working. Reassess and change your plan instead. Be persistent and tenacious. Walk enveloped in faith and repel self-doubt with self-confidence.

In *Think and Grow Rich*, Napoleon Hill says, "Opportunity has spread its wares before you. Step up to the front, select what you want, create your plan, put the plan into action, and follow through with perseverance. "Capitalistic" this much – Capitalistic America ensures every person the opportunity to render useful service, and to collect riches in proportion to the value of the service." Always provide magnificent value. Exceed all expectations when you do.

Universal Law clearly shows that the money earned after executing your organized plan with great success will either carry positive energy, allowing for a wonderful life; or if cutting corners and taking advantage of another person for money is the energy exchange, then that money carries negative energy and the person receiving the money does not know why they are so unhappy. So, simply put, follow the Golden Rule.

Enjoy the opportunities. Enjoy the planning. Enjoy the implementation. Enjoy the success. Enjoy the support you receive personally and professionally along the way. Enjoy making this world a better place for you and everyone else. Enjoy life.

ERIN LEY

About Erin Ley: As Founder and CEO of Onward Productions, Inc., Erin Ley has spent the last 30 years as an Author, Professional Speaker, Personal and Professional Empowerment and Success Coach predominantly around mindset, Vision and Decision. Founder of many influential summits, including "Life On Track," Erin is also the host of the upcoming online streaming T.V. Show "*Life On Track with Erin Ley*," which is all about helping you get into the driver's seat of your own life.

They call Erin "The Miracle Maker!" As a cancer survivor at age twenty-five, single mom of three at age forty-seven, successful Entrepreneur at age fifty, Erin has shown thousands upon thousands across the globe how to become victorious by being focused, fearless, and excited about life and your future! Erin says, "Celebrate life and you'll have a life worth celebrating!"

To see more about Erin and the release of her 4th book "*WorkLuv: A Love Story*" along with her "Life On Track" Course & Coaching Programs, please visit her website.

Author's website: *www.ErinLey.com*
Book Series Website & Author's Bio: *www.The13StepsToRiches.com*

Fatima Hurd

A FOLLOWER DESTINED TO BE A GREAT LEADER

I was always a dreamer, a visionary I had big plans for myself as a child. I wanted to grow up and be my own boss, an author, heck, the first women president; why not!

I used to read any chance I got when I was a kid. Reading became my escape from reality! I loved to lose myself in my books, I had such imagination, and I remember thinking I would be an author someday! The gift my books gave me was freedom and possibility! The stories would come to life, and the possibilities of what I could do with my life were endless!

I learned to become a character in my own story.

In my early twenties, I went through my first transformation, when I lost the weight and got confident and felt empowered because I was making things happen!

At 21, I got a job at the casino. I wanted to work at Caesars Palace. At 25, I got my first management position after I leveled up and went through the "Jump Start Your Future Program" from UNLV from Caesars Palace. I was on fire, as my dearest friend Louisa would say!

I was empowered, but little did I know that I was being groomed for the person I was meant to be!

To which I want to thank my friend and mentor, Hina Reed, who saw something inside of me that, at the time, I could not!

She took me under her wing when I worked with her at Caesars Palace and guided me through peeling back the layers to discover the greatness of the superpowers inside me. When I went through the UNLV program for management, I experienced so many possibilities. I entered a world full of wonder; I had the opportunity to work with some great leaders. As part of my program, I got to explore other positions in hospitality. At 24, I got to experience what it was like to mingle and work with the elite.

I remember catering and opening up credit lines of million dollars or more for our high-end customers! Working alongside Chris Corona and Hina Reed really opened up my world to more possibilities! I was mesmerized by this new world I was invited to be a part of for the next three months as I went through my training. This was when I realized how I enjoyed being of service to others! I remember the million-dollar slot tournaments we would host exclusively for our high- end players, including parties and dinners at high-end restaurants. I remember being intimidated yet showing up because I knew this was where I wanted to be. But even though I was intimidated by the newness of this experience, I did not shy away from it. This career allowed me to grow, and this was just the beginning. Finally, I graduated from the program and got a position in management. I finally outgrew this chapter in my life and was ready to move on to my next assignment. As you may recall from previous chapters, in 2008, I was let go due to staff reductions. I understand now that this was the universe's way of helping me grow.

In *Think and Grow Rich,* Napoleon Hill, mentioned that most great leaders started at the capacity of a follower! This is how my mind interpreted that, I went through the process of being a great employee to learn to become a great business leader!

I find it interesting how at that moment, I was not able to see my potential and the greatness that was lying dormant inside me, but others did!

After this, I went through another transformation, a more humbling experience. One that required me to look inward for peace and answers.

It almost felt like someone hit the CTL-ALT-Del button to restart my life on a clean slate.

I started out as a great employee (intelligent follower) to learn the skills I needed to become a great business leader!

I finally decided to shift from my 9-5 to full-time in my business as a photographer. After doing this for a full year, it just felt right. I was so open and ready to do this!

After a year, my business partner and I had a different vision for the business, and we ended our partnership. I was terrified, but I wasn't quite ready to throw in the towel on my business! For a long time, I struggled with imposter syndrome.

Although I was still honing in my skills as a photographer, I was nowhere near her skill level. However, my exceptional skills in customer service managed to keep me in business. I had no prior experience as a business owner, but I made it work! I still had a vision for myself as a great photographer. At the time, I did not know much about marketing. But I was still able to provide my clients with the best experience ever and slowly build my business solely through word of mouth, with client retention being 100 percent.

After a few months, I went into another partnership with another photographer, and I envisioned creating something amazing. We had different styles and niches of photography, so this amazing plan was to combine our talents to cater to a bigger market. We were such a great team for weddings, quinceañeras, and events! All was going well, and then my husband's company decided to relocate him to California. So we moved to California summer of 2017. My business partner and I attempted to work from two states, but that went south quickly. I ended up closing the doors to the studio after a few months of moving out here.

A quitter never wins- and a winner never quits!

Although I took a break, photography remained a passion that I refused to quit. Photography was life for me; it was an outlet for my creative mind. For me, photography is much more than just snapping a picture. It became my secret power to help others see themselves in the best light and version of themselves. I was photographing lifestyle pictures before they became a thing. When I first started photography, everyone wanted the perfect family outdoor shot where everyone was perfectly poised and looking at the camera. Instead, my clients experience lifestyle photos that tell their stories in a way that embodies who they really are. I was capturing branding photos before they became a thing too. I had a couple that would come to me for their headshots, and I would capture fun, authentic, energized photos that would tell their story as a power couple. And the reason I was able to do this was that I knew and understood what my client's needs were, and they trusted me.

When I moved to California, I convinced myself that I needed to take a break and regroup until I figured it out. Well, that was not the best decision. The longer it took to start my business, the more difficult it became.

My next transformation began after I decided that I was ready to go back into the business. I must have been on high vibration because when I decided to move forward with this, all of a sudden, I was on fire. This began the last year, 2021, when I got in the clubhouse and met Mr. Erik Swanson, "Mr. Awesome!"

I attended my first mastermind, and it was life-changing because I was ready!

After being a member of the Habitude Warrior Mastermind for almost a year, I discovered that my intention in having a business partner wasn't a lack of not knowing how to run a business. It was, at least for me, that I could see the potential when great minds come together, and the possibilities we could create were endless. What I wanted for myself and my business partners was what I found by being a member of the mastermind. I discovered how to be resourceful through borrowed benefits. By borrowing someone else confidence when I needed to, learning from those who were where I wanted to be, and giving value through my experience. This experience helped me grow and transform from an intelligent follower to a great leader! I have seen the growth and shift in my mindset, and now I get to stand for others.

My experience as a member of the Habitude Warriors masterminds led to some great opportunities, such as being part of this amazing book series.

I was creating connections that led to the creation and launch of my Fatima Hurd Brand Photography business. In addition, it has led to creating other business opportunities and, more importantly, to pay it forward and believe in others as I had the blessing with others believing in me.

FATIMA HURD

About Fatima Hurd: Fatima is a personal brand photographer and was featured in the special edition of Beauty & Lifestyle's mommy magazine. Fatima specializes in personal branding photography dedicated to helping influencers and entrepreneurs expand their reach online with strategic, creative, inspiring, and visual content. Owner of a digital consulting agency, Social Branding Photography, Fatima helps professionals with all their digital needs.

Fatima holds ten years of photography experience. An expert in her field, she helps teach photography to middle school students and she hosts workshops to teach anyone who wants to learn how to use and improve their skills with DSLR and on manual mode. Hurd is also a mother of three, wife, certified Reiki master, and certified crystal healer. She loves being out in nature, enjoys taking road trips with her family, and loves meditation and yoga on the beach.

Author's website: *www.FatimaHurd.com*
Book Series Website & Author's Bio: *www.The13StepsToRiches.com*

Frankie Fegurgur

DOES YOUR SYSTEM RUN YOUR BUSINESS?

Nowhere is there more uncertainty and complexity than in military operations. America spends over $700 billion a year maintaining a global presence of over 2 million troops. Organized Planning is embedded in their existence, from aircraft carriers in the Philippine Sea to soldiers training the Iraqi military to the reserve force standing by in all 50 states. They utilize time-tested techniques to create dynamic strategies that address any crisis within hours. While you may not have the budget or manpower of the Department of Defense, you can integrate their systems mentality while becoming the leader that you're meant to be. It's time to translate desire into action!

The crux of military operations is three cyclical elements: Planning, Execution, and Assessment. This translates well for running a business but is seldom adhered to. As an entrepreneur, it's tempting to focus only on execution. You love your product or service and are convinced that everyone will love it too. While that passion is priceless, it quickly becomes resentment as profits wane, bills pile up, and employees burn out. Back when the world was simpler, small businesses could get by on mediocre offerings and hasty business plans. But competition is greater than ever, and anyone still hoping for the pre-2020 'return to normalcy' is likely to fail.

Entrepreneurs should do what generates the highest probability of success. They must create a powerful enough framework to solve problems but flexible enough to evolve. America is a capitalistic country. Banks create money by lending it. That loan becomes an asset for the bank. Whoever can strategically direct the supply and demand of such assets wins. Look at the largest corporations that have reached billions and even trillions of dollars in market value. Do you think they neglect to plan?

Consider the case of Target, which has 2 million customers a day. In 2021, they posted annual revenues of $93 billion! Smooth is fast. Target has a process for each commonly encountered situation. They make shopping frictionless with a free app that can be used in-store to locate items, find coupons and even save payment methods. They designed their own point of sale software and increased wi-fi strength so that registers and handheld devices work faster. They even utilize bots that troubleshoot IT issues to keep the website running strong 24/7. This is all seamless, creating some of the most loyal customers in retail.

While some entrepreneurs will under-plan, most will over-plan. They will worry over minute details and claim to be perfectionists. The truth is often that they are so afraid of failing that they are paralyzed. They may become intimidated by their lack of resources when comparing themselves to Target, Walmart, or Best Buy. If you've ever felt like the underdog, you're not alone. If you've felt off-balance, stagnated, or unsure, I will show you how even a decent plan will be more than enough to materialize your desires. We live in a time of incredible access to technology at an affordable price. Small businesses don't have to feel lost at sea, struggling to tread water. The right systems will eliminate headaches and pump valuable time and capital back into your business. Systems should be as specific and automated as possible. There shouldn't be much decision-making as the workflow has already been determined. When decisions need to be made manually, your staff must feel empowered in real-time. Their success will come down to proper leadership and strong logistics.

This is no easy undertaking, so let's evaluate how the underdog branch of the American military approaches Organized Planning.

The United States Marine Corps is the most powerful military force in the entire world. While they have a complex hierarchy of planning methods, they maintain their dominance by a surprisingly simple approach: brilliance in the basics. Decentralized, small group leadership is expressed through massive action, generating confidence and camaraderie. This action is aligned with the commander's intent, becoming more specific as it approaches the boots on the ground. Each person knows their role and how it fits in with the overall mission. They train exactly how they will perform, focusing only on what they can control. I've lived this ethos firsthand. As I mentioned in Volume 1, I served as a Marine in many roles, with each promotion bringing me deeper into the planning process. The scope of worldwide operations is immense beyond belief, and I felt privileged to learn from true leaders. For the first time ever, I'm going to condense and distill the lessons learned from my career into a barebones, stay-in-the-heart-of-the-action version that you can put to work today. Here are the six steps:

1. Frame the problem
2. Draft solutions
3. Sandbox each solution
4. Rework the best solution
5. Implement risk management
6. Deploy solution and monitor results

The first step is to frame the problem. It doesn't matter how great your plan is if you don't truly understand the problem. This will illuminate why the problem must be solved. The second step is to create potential solutions. Don't try to create the one magic solution, as there is no way to know what will work in the real world. That's where the sandbox comes in. Test each solution in a controlled environment and compare the results. Go back to the drawing board and rework the best solution until it is viable. Again, it won't be perfect. Step 5 is critical because risks can never be fully removed in the real world. As a leader, you must avoid unnecessary risk and minimize the effects of inherent risk. Just as each Marine is a leader, each staff member must feel safe enough to speak up when there is a safety concern. The final step is to deploy your plan and collect feedback with the buy-in of your mastermind and your staff.

Your mastermind group will make or break your business. Leadership is an art as much as it is a science. This roundtable of generals won't follow you unless you're the real deal. Of course, they'll expect compensation, networking opportunities, and more. You'll need to demonstrate that not only do you understand the problem that you're solving, but you also know the proper sequencing of action. Get their feedback at each step because differing perspectives will unlock a level of clarity that you wouldn't otherwise have access to. This is especially true when members of your mastermind aren't from the same industry as you. Learn to accept feedback graciously. Don't be so in love with the plan that you go down with the ship.

Now that the plan is launched, it must be adhered to until it's too dangerous or obsolete. Unfortunately, people have grown accustomed to trying a plan only once or twice before giving up. Decide in advance the time and resources you're committing to deploy. Remember that the longer and more complex the plan, the more room for ambiguity. Sometimes simple and decisive is best. Present your plan with absolute certainty. Visual aids are important but don't overly rely on them or recite them verbatim. Now is the time to look your people in the eyes and transfer your belief to them. Facilitate conversations across departments and responsibilities. Don't let grumblings grow over which workgroups have it easier or better than others. People tend to fool themselves into believing that they are the hardest working person they know, causing problems in the absence of collaboration.

Your mastermind and staff will follow your every move. They will see how you treat people and behave when you think no one is watching. Napoleon Hill provides an extensive self-evaluation of traits of effective and ineffective leaders. I challenge you to not only rate yourself but also have your mastermind rate you. I was once asked which traits of leaders are most important. The two that are referenced in both Marine Corps doctrine and *Think and Grow Rich* are justice and judgment. You lose all credibility when you allow a few to be above reproach. When the well-being of your staff and the success of the plan are in your hands, can you be relied upon to make the proper decision based on the information you have in front of you?

Bring your team to the table, and ensure they are well compensated in more ways than just financially. Value and expect their input and empower them to act independently. Observe trends and anticipate obstacles. Remember that a plan shouldn't be carved in stone; it should be drawn on a whiteboard. The format is irrelevant in comparison to the content. Your team will learn to trust your judgment and your confidence. This doesn't require the biggest budget or the shiniest equipment. In fact, for over 246 years, America's Marines have always done more with less and wouldn't have it any other way.

FRANKIE FEGURGUR

About Frankie Fegurgur: Frankie's "burning desire" is helping people retire with dignity. Frankie distills the lessons he has learned over the last 15 years and empowers our youth to make better financial decisions than the generation before them. This is a deeply personal mission for him—he was born to high-school-aged parents, and money was always a struggle. Frankie learned that hard work, alone, wasn't the key to financial freedom and sought a more fulfilling path. Now, he serves as the COO of a nonprofit financial association based in the San Francisco Bay Area, teaching money mindfulness. He, his wife, and their two children can be found exploring, volunteering, and building throughout their community.

Author's website: *www.FrankMoneyTalk.com*
Book Series Website & Author's Bio: *www.The13StepsToRiches.com*

Fred Moskowitz

REACHING YOUR DESTINATIONS

The notion of this sixth step of Organized Planning revolves around the crystallization of desire into action. This recalls the idea that we should always "begin with the end in mind." In other words, it is a best practice to make sure that we are clear about what it is that we want and that we have a concrete goal or objective before we begin our action.

This process of Organized Planning can be summarized in the following steps:

1. Get clarity on your goal or objective and internalize why that goal is important to you.

2. Break down that goal into smaller milestones or mini-goals. Assign a definitive time for each step. Arrange the goals as needed while considering if anything is dependent on completing an earlier milestone.

3. Determine and identify any outside resources or support you will need. Surround yourself with others seeking like-minded goals using the Mastermind Principle.

4. Set realistic timeframes and be open to adjusting as you go.

5. Get organized and develop a written schedule by which you will put in consistent effort. Apply a strong work ethic to this schedule and establish points at which you will periodically review your progress as you go.

Getting Clarity

For a quick assessment, you may find it helpful to start by asking yourself some of the following questions.

- Does your objective have a descriptive "definition of done" that you would be able to easily describe or convey to someone else verbally?

- How do you know that you have successfully achieved your goal?

- What does achieving that goal look like to you?

Taking some thinking time to consider these questions can have a major impact on your organized planning, as well as on your success in achieving your goals.

Let's say that you were about to embark on a long car trip to reach an exciting vacation destination. You would certainly look on a map to identify your starting point and destination point and plan your route. Alternatively, you might input the destination address into your GPS or smartphone. Imagine what would happen if, instead, you were to simply begin driving on the highway and making turns randomly without having done that first step. You would certainly find yourself getting lost and covering a lot of extra ground.

Specificity is another quality to strive for, and it also goes hand in hand with clarity. Therefore, it is vital that we are specific about what we want and our goals.

For instance, if you find that you are hungry one afternoon and were to call up your local pizza shop, they would answer the phone and ask what you would like. Responding with a vague answer such as "I'm hungry" or "I want some food" will certainly irritate the employee and will result in a rude response in a louder voice, such as "Well, whaddya want?". As I envision this theoretical banter in my mind, I can just imagine how the accentuation and nuance might even be significantly more pronounced if this were taking place in New York City.

On the other hand, if you were to be very specific and clear, and ask for a large pizza with mushrooms, along with a garden salad with Italian dressing on the side, then exactly what you asked for would show up being delivered to your doorstep within ten minutes.

What is your "WHY"?

Although this is a very common question, it is also a very powerful one. As we learned in Volume Two of this book series about the important step of DESIRE, we know that having a burning desire is crucial to obtaining anything that is of major importance to us. And a large part of the energy associated with having a burning desire is knowing our "WHY." Having a clear "WHY" gives us our sense of purpose. This also gives us our motivation, guiding light, and inspiration to keep pushing ahead even when times are tough.

Some examples of answers to this question may revolve around more than one of the following:

- Achieving success
- Overcoming adversity or hardship in life
- Inspiring others in life
- Taking care of my family
- Leaving a legacy for the future
- Making an impact

In *Think and Grow Rich*, recall when Napoleon Hill tells us the story about how Thomas Edison failed 9,999 times at creating a working electric light bulb before he came up with the successful version. Working in his laboratory in Menlo Park, New Jersey, Edison needed to use his PERSISTENCE to work and test thousands and thousands of different materials for his incandescent light bulb. This is a wonderful example of how a burning DESIRE, a clear WHY, and PERSISTENCE all come together, resulting in a creation that has changed the world.

The Value of a Mastermind

The value and benefits of participating in a Mastermind group are not to be overlooked. In fact, Napoleon Hill further goes on to highlight this point by declaring that compliance with this instruction is *absolutely essential.*

Mastermind groups and alliances can take on many forms and configurations. The commonality among them is the idea that like-minded people are coming together to work together on a common or shared goal. Masterminds may be made up of individuals who are all in the same line of business or industry, or they may come from diverse areas of commerce and business. They may be paid membership groups or free. The depth of experience among the participants can vary all the way from an inexperienced new person up to an industry veteran with decades of experience. The group members are always ready to bring value and generously give of their knowledge and expertise to help others.

In *Think and Grow Rich,* Hill describes the Mastermind principle as "the coordination of knowledge and effort between two or more people who work towards a definite purpose in a spirit of harmony...no two minds ever come together without thereby creating a third, invisible, intangible force, which may be likened to a third mind."

Having participated in many different mastermind groups throughout my career, I have benefited tremendously from the counsel and guidance shared with me. This *intangible force* can take on many forms: it may be an idea, providing feedback or an alternative perspective, a solution to a problem from someone who has experienced it, an introduction to a new contact, or sharing a resource. In addition, I have been able to help and support countless other people throughout those mastermind groups. This is the experience of the law of reciprocity at work - when you give of yourself freely to others, it will eventually come back to you multiple times over. Usually, it will show up from a completely different source than where you directed your efforts.

Summary

In this chapter, we have discussed some of the key steps in setting up your organized planning. This is one of the longest chapters in Think and Grow Rich, and it certainly warrants the most attention and focus. It contains all the information you will need to achieve your goals and objectives.

Getting Clarity - Spend time performing a self-assessment and getting clear on what you want to accomplish.

Determine Your "WHY" - Having a clear sense of purpose will keep you motivated when times are tough and keep you well-grounded all throughout your journey.

The Power of Association - The act of creating alliances with like-minded people and forming a collective will create an intangible force where the sum is greater than each of its individual parts.

As you make progress on your journey, I encourage you to keep a journal so that you can remember all your wins and keep track of all the ways in which you've improved. I have found that taking a few minutes each day to write down your top three wins literally and celebrate them will give you amazing results. Write down the small wins, as well as the big ones. This serves to keep you feeling good, keeps you in the spirit of gratitude and serves as a constant reminder that you are building momentum every single day.

FRED MOSKOWITZ

About Fred Moskowitz: Fred Moskowitz is a best-selling author, investment fund manager, and speaker who is on a personal mission to teach people about the power of investing in alternative asset classes, such as real estate and mortgage notes, showing them the way to diversify their capital into investments that are uncorrelated from Wall Street and the stock markets.

Through his body of work, he is teaching investors the strategies to build passive income and cash flow streams designed to flow into their bank accounts. He's a frequent event speaker and contributor to investment podcasts.

Fred is the author of *The Little Green Book of Note Investing: A Practical Guide for Getting Started with Investing in Mortgage Notes* and contributing author in *1Habit To Thrive in a Post-Covid World.*

Author's Website: *www.FredMoskowitz.com*
Book Series Website & Author's Bio: *www.The13StepsToRiches.com*

Gina Bacalski

DISCOVERING MY TRIBE

I had just finished my first full-length novel. Struggling with imposter syndrome, I searched for what to do next. I gobbled up all podcasts, panels, workshops, and classes I could find. After I stumbled into the Brandon Sanderson's Podcast, Writing Excuses' panel at Utah's version of Comic-Con called FanX, one of the panelists and podcast founding member, Howard Taylor, told the audience something that I would never forget.

"If you have written a novel, guess what? You're a writer!"

I took a moment and let that sink in. I had, after all, just completed my first novel. Did that I mean that I was really a writer? Could I truly lay claim to such an illustrious title? His words echoed in my head again, "If you have written a novel, guess what? You're a writer!" I felt a rush of excitement and alleviation. I have written a novel! I am a writer! Howard Taylor said so. I listened more closely to the panel for my next steps.

Time and time again, the whole panel referenced their writing groups as being an integral part of their writing process. They talked about how having a writing group made all the difference in their own personal writing. Brandon Sanderson reiterated how that was how he began his success and how he still leans on this writing group to this day.

I knew what I needed now. A writing group! Fantastic! Now, where did I find one of those?

After a short yet thorough search, I was not satisfied with the results. So I researched what a writing group should be, but I did not find anything that fit my needs and requirements. So I decided to create my own.

I found a writing class at my local library. I quickly enrolled and eagerly attended the first meeting. Then I listened. Yes, to the teacher, but more importantly to the questions my classmates were asking the teacher. Each week I sat in a different location and studied my peers as much as I studied the material.

With two classes left, I had made my choices. In my research and after listening to Writing Excuses and using that as a guide, I wanted a writing group that wrote many different genres, apart from my preferred genres to write (which are Romance, Fantasy, and Inspirational), so I asked questions and listened more. Finally, I officially introduced myself, explained what I was looking to start, and collected contact information.

Including my friend Scott whom I had met previously at church, I had successfully collected a fellow romance writer, a YA Sci-Fi/fantasy writer, a graphic novel/non-fiction historical writer, an autobiographical writer, and a comic strip writer. I was very pleased with the diversity.

The last class came to an end, and we set up a time to formally meet, and I put us all in a text group chat.

During our first meeting, we set up the rules and submission schedules, named ourselves (the Pensive Scribblers), set writing goals, and went to work!

Although there have been a few bumps along the way and new schedules that needed to be arranged over time, it has been a little under five years, and we are still meeting regularly. When someone learns something new about writing or the writing process, we will hold a special writing group and share the information we learned with the entire group.

We also have an annual Halloween Party, in which we write and share spooky short fiction, and an annual Christmas Party to celebrate all that we have accomplished that year.

Since we started, several members have completed works, others have had the proper encouragement to take on extremely challenging projects, and three of us have become published.

I rely on my Pensive Scribblers with everything I write, including these 13 Steps to Riches chapters. They are my writing tribe, my writing family. We mastermind all sorts of book scenarios and ideas. We have helped each other grow as writers in ways that I can't put into words. Their feedback, advice, and critiques have become invaluable to me, and I can't imagine writing anything in earnest without them.

Just like I needed a writing group, when I switched careers and acquired my real estate license, I realized I was in need again. For the first time in my career, especially after such a drastic career change (from Childcare Expert to Real Estate Agent), I needed to be surrounded by others like me. I needed to be surrounded by business leaders and rock star entrepreneurs.

Again, I found myself looking for a group of true peers to surround myself with. I tried out every networking group I could find or got an invitation to. I met many fantastic people and found a lot of interesting ideologies, but nothing really fit as well as I'd hoped for.

I was contemplating starting my own networking group, and then I walked into a group called Amplified Minds, and I met Jon Kovach Jr. and Levi McPhearson, and I was completely blown away. The way they did networking was different. I felt like I was finally surrounded by my actual peers, creating real relationships and getting tangible feedback to help with my issues and problems. In turn, I felt inspired to give advice on things that others needed help with and connect them with people I knew who could better help them solve their problems.

And that, ladies and gentlemen, is magic.

I went to every mastermind session I could; I did all the activities, and I started to surround myself with as many of those amazing people as I could. I became friends with Levi, and he has become a mentor to me in many aspects of my life.

Jon and I became and have remained very close as well, and I often joked about Jon being my "work husband." I was incredibly blessed to have been one of his chosen few to sit down and hash out what would become Champion Circle, Jon's new mastermind group that Amplified Minds evolved into.

Through Champion Circle and the brilliant masterminds that we created there and the studying of Napoleon Hill's books and other works as a group, I was able to triple my real estate business.

The system of reading and learning together, talking about it, and then meeting to help each other mastermind that Jon and I came up with was incredibly inspiring. In the mastermind group, we lifted each other with knowledge and applicable business help. I explored several books that I didn't even know I needed until I devoured them with my group of peers. I learned new ways to do things and new ways to think by consuming some of the classics and new and inspired thoughts.

My husband joined me in those sessions, and applying what we learned has helped our marriage and relationship become even better. We have our masterminds now about family issues and challenges. We continue to read books together and have a meaningful exchange about what we have learned and how and what we would like to be applied to our family dynamic.

I guess the point of all this is that if there isn't a group ready to embrace you, make your own! Find your people, and then build your tribe. Make sure you have the people around you who will lift you up and help you achieve your goals.

Imagine what would happen if everyone applied these principles. What if everyone came together and had conversations and actually tried to help each other solve problems and concerns? What if everyone tried to bring positivity to help one another, both in business and personal matters? Imagine if we could come together to create instead of competing. How much better would our outcomes be? How much better would YOUR outcomes be?

GINA BACALSKI

About Gina Bacalski: Gina is a Real Estate Agent, licensed since June 2018. Her background is in Early Childhood Education where she received her Child Development Associate from the state of Utah and has an AS from BYU-Idaho. For the past seventeen years, Gina has thoroughly enjoyed her experience in the service industry helping families in the gifted community.

In 2019, Gina helped Jon Kovach Jr. launch Champion Circle and is now CEO of the organization. She brings her genuine love for people, high attention to detail, and strives to exceed client's expectations to the Real Estate industry and to Champion Circle.

Gina married the man of her dreams, Jay Bacalski, in San Diego, in 2013. The Bacalskis love entertaining friends and family, going on hikes, and attending movies and plays. When Gina isn't helping her clients navigate the real estate world, she will most often be found dancing and listening to BTS, watching KDramas and writing fantasy, sci-fi and romance novels.

Author's Website: *www.MyChampionCircle.com/Gina-Bacalski*
Book Series Website & Author's Bio: *www.The13StepstoRiches.com*

Griselda Beck

THE SUBTLE ART OF MAKING STUFF HAPPEN!

Organized Planning: the art of execution. In our last book on Imagination, I shared with you about permitting yourself to let your dreams run wild, envisioning a new possibility better than the one at this moment. In this chapter, we get to look at how we make those dreams a reality! To create these, we need to understand the problem we are solving and have a clear vision and solid strategy, including contingency planning and rigor, commitment, and urgency.

Let's break it down.

The Problem. I remember feeling trapped years ago. Every day seemed to be more of the same: putting out fires, sustained by caffeine and adrenaline. My dream job had become this cyclical Groundhog Day. I felt like a hamster on a wheel running nowhere fast and burning out. Some days I felt like a Zombie, hollow and dead inside, just going through the motions. I blamed everyone and everything, including my then partner, coworkers, and family.

I eventually got to face the hard truth: I was 100% responsible for my unhappiness. After experiencing a health crisis, I had a wake-up call that something had to change. I had to change.

The problem was that I didn't know what the problem was, or so that is how I felt at the time. After all, I had the job I always wanted and worked so hard to get. I was making great money and had so much to be thankful for, yet I wasn't "happy."

Feeling stuck and completely lost for the first time in my life, I sought support from a therapist and a life coach. The problem was that in pursuit of my "dream job" and goals, I lost sight of my whole self; everything else that also made me happy, and no longer made time for many things I enjoyed. I had the financial freedom I worked so hard for, but I wasn't sleeping much, having fun, and I wasn't being present in my relationships, so love felt so distant, and I felt lonely.

The Vision. I wanted to travel, go on adventures on random days of the week, dance and sing my heart out, have passionate wild sex, feel madly in love, experience closeness, and feel loved in all of my significant relationships romantic, family, and friends. I wanted to LOVE my LIFE! I wanted to feel safe, loved, joyful, and connected in all areas of my life.

We began exploring possibilities that would enable me to live the life I desired in my "ideal world" design. It took a lot of "just humor me" moments from my coach to get to that design because I was so stuck at the time on how life "just is" and how "that's just not realistic." Still, I played along and designed a "fantasy life" in the form of journaling, declarations, affirmations, vision boarding, dreaming, and thinking, "wouldn't it be nice if…".

Eventually, I got to a clear picture of what life would look like if "I had no one else to think about," "I was guaranteed everything I requested would be a YES," and "if tomorrow was my last day, how would I spend today." AND most importantly, how I would FEEL if I got to experience life that way.

"I don't want to be tied to a physical address!" I yelled out in frustration as I answered the key transformation question. What do you want? For what felt like the thousandth time (probably actually only the 10th time). Followed by "I would feel FREE!" Freedom is what I craved. Freedom was the destination!

Freedom in the form of flexibility of time and location was missing from my career so that I could do all of the things I previously listed! WOW! That truth unlocked the path to where I am today. I didn't want a job that I lived for. I wanted a job that allowed me to live. This very simple shift in perspective changed everything!

Strategy. "Changing my life" to create freedom was no small task.

It took lots of planning, starting with a gap analysis on what was between me and where I wanted to be to identify the core pieces that needed to be changed. The first was my job. I looked at all of the possibilities, renegotiating my current job for more flexibility of schedule and location, checking out other jobs, and choosing the option I would ultimately choose: a total career change. This change took commitment, rigor, urgency, contingency planning, and agility.

Contingency Planning. Evaluate the risks and vulnerable points in your plan so that you can evaluate alternative solutions. One example in this story was, "what if I don't start making money right away?" I set myself up to be able to receive income from multiple sources and have a safety net in the form of savings, ample credit line availability, and liquid assets that were easily accessible should I get myself in a pinch. This was like having my own bank for myself! Be sure to set yourself up for success and give yourself options.

Rigor. Being connected to the details and periodically revisiting your current status concerning your goal is being in a "relationship with your results." Keeping your eye on the goal while understanding the details and progress towards key milestones is a critical component of organized planning to ensure successful outcomes. Many people avoid this step because they don't want to experience "failure," accountability, and change. Avoidance can cost a lot of wasted time and money: set goals that are measurable and milestones or periodic checkpoints for evaluating your progress and results.

Urgency. Doing the above will set you up for success in URGENCY (proactive) vs. emergency (reactive). This is the antidote to Procrastination. Take committed action now. A periodic planning exercise is a way to set yourself up for success that has worked for my clients and me. I like to do this weekly; some do it daily. This "weekly planning" process is how I ensure that my calendar matches my commitments. It enables me to foresee where I might need to renegotiate previous commitments to make room for emerging priorities and deconflict competing priorities before it becomes an emergency, which requires more time (plus a lot of guilt, shame, and frustration) to clean up and clear.

Agility. As I always tell my clients when they hit slumps and bumps in the road, "Life will always keep LIFE-ing" and present you with circumstances outside your control. Being rigorous in evaluating your results, gap, and options when these unexpected interruptions and barriers occur, enables you to see possibilities and make powerful choices. In short, this means don't "Set it and Forget it." Autopilot mode is a buzzkill for an extraordinary life. Remain committed to your plan yet flexible and rigorous so that you can make powerful choices and take action quickly.

Commitment. See it through no matter what. There will be times (perhaps even a LOT of times) when you notice you're off track; your results are not as expected, or you feel like you've failed. Most people at this point take these results personally and will wallow in the feelings of guilt, shame, and blame and the resulting aftermath of that. Instead, train yourself to default to:

Acknowledge it Give yourself grace

Ask yourself, "What worked? What didn't work? What action am I committed to next?"

Relentless Resilience is a muscle that can be trained. I refer to it in my coaching practice when working with entrepreneurs as your "CEO Muscle." Know your results and know YOU are not your results.

Embracing these two truths allows the clear space to remain objective and take necessary actions to pivot, recover or redirect the plan to accomplish your goal. Whatever you feel, do, or encounter, NEVER GIVE UP if you really desire it. It's only ever over when you say you're done. Everything else is "figureoutable."

GRISELDA BECK

About Griselda Beck: Griselda Beck, M.B.A. is a powerhouse motivational speaker and coach who combines her executive expertise with transformational leadership, mindset, life coaching, and heart-centered divine feminine energy principles. Griselda empowers women across the globe to step into their power, authenticity, hearts, and sensuality, to create incredible success in their business and freedom in their lives. She creates confident CEOs.

Griselda's clients have experienced success in quitting their 9-5 jobs, tripling their rates, getting their first clients, launching their first products, and growing their businesses in a way that allows them to live the lifestyles and freedoms they want. She has been featured as a top expert on *FOX, ABC, NBC, CBS, MarketWatch, Telemundo*, and named on the Top 10 Business Coaches list by *Disrupt Magazine*.

Griselda is an executive with over 15 years of corporate experience, founder of Latina Boss Coach and Beck Consulting Group, and serves as president for the nonprofit organization MANA de North County San Diego. She also volunteers her time teaching empowerment mindset at her local homeless shelter, Operation Hope-North County.

Author's Website: *www.LatinaBossCoach.com*
Book Series Website & Author's Bio: *www.The13StepstoRiches.com*

Jason Curtis

LIKE A BOAT WITHOUT A RUDDER

Hill stated, "The successful leader must plan his work and work his plan. A leader who moves by guesswork without practical definite plans is comparable to a ship without a rudder. Sooner or later, he will land on the rocks."

"...A ship without a rudder." This is so true! If you don't make a plan, you can certainly plan on failing. There have been countless examples of this in my life. One example was when I was transitioning out of the Navy. I knew that I wanted to continue my federal service, which has ultimately led me to my current position. I have the honor of helping US Veterans receive the benefits that they are so richly deserving.

Daily Habits For Success

My best daily habit that allows me to be successful in this principle of Organized Planning is to make a plan to accomplish the tasks necessary in everything that I need to.

One vital thing to understand is that having a plan does not mean success. It would be best to be ready for any plan to fail and adjust appropriately.

Advice To A Younger Me

There are many steps to planning, and the sooner you can understand and implement them, the better you'll accomplish what you planned.

Failing to plan is problem number one. But failing to work out the plan is problem number two. Too often, when a plan is developed, it is set aside after serving the initial purpose of envisioning the business or securing capital. That is undoubtedly valuable, but the maximum value comes afterward from working on the plan.

Techniques In Maintaining Organizational Planning Skills

I used to maintain organized planning because I know planning is cyclical and continuous. What I mean is this:

1. Envision the end state. Before any plan can be drafted, you have to envision what you want at the end of it all.
2. Assess the Current State – Once we have envisioned the end state, we are eager to get going, either moving straight to the execution phases (for which there is no plan) or jumping into planning without taking a complete inventory of the current situation.
3. Agree on the Gap – Effective mastermind groups and problem-solving techniques such as Design Thinking seek to avoid the temptation of problem-solving before consensus on what the problem is.
4. Devise a Plan to Close the Gap – Now you are ready to develop the plan. Plans don't have to be lengthy and complex, but they must be actionable. Hill says this about them: "The most intelligent man living cannot succeed in accumulating money – nor in any other undertaking – without practical and workable plans."
5. Execute the Plan – If all you do is develop a plan, there is some value because you have at least critically thought about the end state and the path forward, so now it is part of your psyche, even if buried somewhere in the recesses of your mind.

My Mentors

Think of some of your mentors you have learned from through the years. Do you have any stories you can share from your experiences by learning to step out of your comfort zone and apply this particular step-to-riches principle?

Keep in mind that you may not have noticed you were applying it at the time, but looking back now, it's very clear. Share that! Readers love that!

Just about any mentor I've ever had has stressed the importance of planning. My first mentor, Michael Marcial, taught me this not long ago. Without his help, I wouldn't be where I am today!

Surprises

The biggest surprise in my journey, the more that I had a plan, the more likely I was to succeed.

But then, on the other hand, if I didn't have a plan, I would most certainly fail.

I tend to face adversity and obstacles head-on. Being honest and upfront in tackling the hard things in life is particularly helpful in overcoming adversity and obstacles for me.

My secret weapon and advice are to become a planner in all that you do. Without planning, you will end up like a ship without a rudder.

Best Counsel To Up-leveling Yourself

I would counsel anyone who wants to up-level to find a mentor or a person willing to teach them.

Another concept that can have an immediate impact is to surround yourself with others that will challenge you and help you emulate the qualities you want to have in your life.

Set Up Your Day For Ultimate Success

Former North Carolina State head basketball coach Jimmy Valvano said it best, "If you think, you laugh, and you cry, that's a heckuva day." These straightforward yet profound actions have significantly impacted my life and can impact yours.

JASON CURTIS

About Jason Curits: Jason has been a serial entrepreneur for 15 years and has enjoyed serving and helping his fellow entrepreneurs build their businesses and win in this game of life—on purpose! Jason created On Purpose Coaching because he knew, through his life experiences, that he could create an impact in others. He focuses on helping his clients create better relationships with their customers. This fosters trust and rapport while generating customer loyalty.

Jason is a Navy veteran of six years. He has sailed the seas and oceans in serving his God and country. Curtis and his wife, Brianna, have been married for eight years, and they have two children.

Author's Website: *www.JasonLaneCurtis.com*
Book Series Website & Author's Bio: *www.The13StepstoRiches.com*

Jeffrey Levine

PLANNING IS THE KEY

In March of my senior year of college, I woke up one morning and thought to myself, "What am I going to do after I graduate?" Since I didn't have a family business to go into, and I didn't really have any special skills for a job, I panicked. Then I remembered my next-door neighbor, a lawyer, who had a great lifestyle. So I purchased a book about applying to law school; it was really thick and listed every law school in the US.

Initially, I remembered almost every law school had a cut-off date of March 1 for applying. I planned to review every option in my book to see if any offered admission after March 1. Regretfully, I didn't find any. I was heartbroken because I felt as if a door had been closed.

Since many schools were listed in the book, I thought I might have missed one that would take my application. I initiated plan B: to review the book again. After spending many hours studying the book on law school admissions, I finally found one I had overlooked the first time. This school had an April 1 deadline. I applied and was accepted.

I knew law school would be a challenging experience for me. That fact became really apparent when, at orientation, the dean stated, "Look to your right and look to your left. At least one of you will not be here at the end of the year."

Because of what the dean said, I needed to design a plan to make it through the first year. I realized it would be helpful to study with another classmate. That's when I met Roy. He was one of the top students and was very open to studying together. Since we both stayed on campus over Christmas break at the school, we studied together. That was very helpful to me because Roy always had answers to all of my questions. With his help, we both passed. Even though 40% of the class flunked, we both made it to the finish line.

After graduating from law school with a very good class ranking, I decided to apply for a graduate law degree in taxation. Because I had done very well in my tax courses in law school and my professor wrote a great reference, I was accepted. However, I knew that the next step would be another challenge because the students were often from the top of their law school classes, and to pass, students needed an average of 80%, rather than the 70% average required in law school.

I needed to design a plan to pass and excel in the taxation program. Thinking about how having a study partner in law school had worked so well, I decided to repeat that approach. I found Tom, and by working together, we both finished in the top 20% of our class.

Next, it was time to apply for a job. With my advanced degree in taxation, I thought getting a job as a tax lawyer would be fairly easy. Unfortunately, I was in for a rude awakening. My applications were rejected everywhere. I needed a different approach. I decided to start networking my way to a job opportunity. Anytime I was invited to a function, I would say yes. After doing that for a few months, it finally worked.

One night, I was invited to play basketball with some friends. At the end of the night, one of my friends shared that his financial planning firm had just lost its tax attorney and was looking to hire one as soon as possible. He suggested that if I were to drop a résumé at the firm first thing the next morning, I would have a good chance of getting the job. I did so, received a call within hours, and an interview was set up. Since my friend said the firm liked people who worked long hours, I emphasized that at my interview and was hired the next day.

After working two years at that firm and getting national tax and financial planning experience, I decided to open my own firm. My plan was to do seminars, get on radio shows, and do TV interviews. Unfortunately, even though I did all of that, I could not grow my practice and struggled to keep the doors open.

Faced with monthly bills that far exceeded my income, I faced a real financial challenge. My new plan was to start networking again. It had worked in the past to find a job, and I felt it could work to gain traction for my business and generate referrals. Through networking, I met accountants and attorneys who referred my business. After a while, I had more quality clients, and my income was more than my expenses. For many years, I had a very successful business.

Then one day, while working out at the gym, a lady tapped me on the shoulder and said her partners wanted to talk to me about a buyout, and they wanted to meet the next day. At our meeting, I was offered a price that I accepted immediately. My next plan was retirement.

My retirement plan was simple. I was going to move to Arizona to be with my son and play golf and enjoy my golden years under the golden sunshine. But, after relaxing and playing golf for four years, I realized I needed to adjust my plan. I needed to do something more than just play golf and be retired. The plan was to partner with another person to do some book writing and speeches. I really didn't know how that would happen, but I felt it was the right plan.

I went to a conference in Orlando, Florida. Even though the event didn't start until Friday night, I arrived Thursday. On that first night, I went to the ballroom to see if I could register. I realized quickly that I was too early for registration. However, there was one book sitting on the table, The Power of Vibration by Don Boyer. I started reading and couldn't put it down. I read the book from cover to cover for the next hour or so.

I loved the book so much that I decided I must meet the author, Don Boyer. As luck would have it, the keynote speaker on Saturday was Don Boyer himself. I was mesmerized by his talk and was eager to connect with him. Even though a long line of people had questions for him after his talk, I waited patiently to introduce myself and get his card.

A few weeks later, I called Don. He said that was the perfect time to speak since he had just pulled into his driveway and was home, where he could get reception. Had I called five minutes earlier, Don would have missed the call.

We eventually authored books together, did documentaries, and even shared some business opportunities. It worked out perfectly.

Once you set a plan to do something, it may not always work out the way you want it to. However, the good news is that you can change the plan to meet the changing circumstances. Remember, you plan for the big events in your life: vacation, wedding, or even a birthday party. So give your life the same consideration. Then, when you create a plan that your life will be the best it can be, you'll set yourself up to make that plan a reality.

JEFFREY LEVINE

About Jeffrey Levine: Jeffrey is a highly skilled tax planner and business strategist, as well as a published author and sought-after speaker. He's been featured in national magazines, on the cover of *Influential People Magazine*, and is a frequent featured expert on radio, talk shows, and documentaries. Jeffrey attended the prestigious Albany Academy for high school and then went on to University of Hartford at Connecticut, University of Mississippi Law School, Boston University School of Law, and earned an L.L.M. in taxation. His accolades include features in *Kiplinger* and *Family Circle Magazine*, as well as a dedicated commentator for Channel 6 and 13 news shows, a contributor for the *Albany Business Review*, and an announcer for WGY Radio.

Jeffrey has accumulated more than 30 years of experience as a tax attorney and certified financial planner and has given in excess of 500 speeches nationally. Levine is the executive producer and cast member in the documentary *Beyond the Secret: The Awakening*.

Levine's most current work, *Consistent Profitable Growth Map*, is a step-by-step workbook outlining easy-to-follow steps to convert consistent revenue growth to any business platform.

Author's Website: *www.JeffreyLevine.Solutions*
Book Series Website & Author's Bio: *www.The13StepstoRiches.com*

Lacey & Adam Platt

LET'S MAKE A PLAN &
THE PLAN WON'T WORK UNLESS YOU DO

Let's Make A Plan

In this book series, we first started by talking about Desire. You must know what you want and then create a desire to achieve it. Then we added on a heaping spoonful of Faith. We need to find strength by believing in a force beyond our own. This was followed by the ability to speak to ourselves positively, which lifts us up through Autosuggestion. Next, we added a sprinkle of Specialized Knowledge by deciding whether we like to have knowledge taught to us or if we like to surround ourselves with those who know the answers that can help us. And then the pizzazz happened! We dug deep inside our childlike brains, remembered what it was like to have imagination, and learned why those with imagination get ahead in life. Now comes the point in which we take all these elements and organize them into a system and plan for our futures!

Organized Planning. Now, remember that it is to your benefit to develop a plan that involves other people. (We will dive into that in a later book all about Masterminds). Because when we try to do things on our own, we have to struggle through each step. When we learn from others, we can skip all of the mistakes and just move on to success. I love the quote by Tony Robbins that says, "Success leaves tracks." Tony means that successful people do things differently, and if we can learn the things they do differently, we can also be successful in a much quicker way and without all the mistakes! Doesn't that sound fantastic?

I mean, sure, we will make mistakes, and the first plan we come up with isn't going to be the final one. It may take several drafts of your plan to find one that actually leads to success. But, the really cool part about finding a plan that leads to success is that now you have the blueprint, and you can do it again and again!

Remember that the joy in life comes from the journey, not the destination. Each plan you devise will take you down a path that will help you create your journey. It may have several bumps or dips or even switchbacks along the way, but the most AMAZING part is it's your journey, and no two peoples look the same. Own it!

Your journey is uniquely designed for you specifically! It is the one path that will lead you to become who you need to be to achieve success! Read that sentence again several times. Do you understand its meaning? There is only one path that will lead you to success. It does not mean you can only be successful one time because once you are successful, you can achieve success over and over again. Ponder on that for a moment and think about it as it pertains to your life and the journey you've taken thus far. Have you become someone different? I used to beat myself up by saying things like, "I thought I would be further than this by this time in my life" or "If I had only done this sooner or instead, I would have been successful years ago." The thing is, I was not yet who I needed to Be. I had not learned all the lessons or experienced all the experiences I needed to mold me into the shape I needed to Be in for that next level. Don't devalue your journey by comparing it to others. Honor where and who you are NOW and know that you are right where you're supposed to be. Keep moving forward!

I read a meme the other day that said, "People often fail because they look at how far they still have to go instead of focusing on how far they've come." Just know that the journey you are taking is of your choosing.

Every moment you make a choice. Are there times when we make a bad choice? Yes! Are there times when we make a good choice? Yes! Each one of those choices molds us into who we Become. If you don't like who you are Becoming, make different choices. So what? It really is that simple. Here's to making great choices!

In the second half of this book series, we will be talking about the last half of the steps that it takes to achieve success and riches. We've already taken five steps (which I summed up for you in the first paragraph). We just added this one, where we organized what we've learned so far. Now when we add the last seven, we will create an equation for riches! You are on your way! Celebrate it!

~ Lacey Platt

The Plan Won't Work Unless You Do

So you have a desire for more. You have faith it will work out; you've invested in yourself and learned what you need to get your desire. Now what? It's time to plan.

I love the part in the last Harry Potter movie when Harry figures out the last Horcrux is at Hogwarts school, and Harry wants to go right now and find it and destroy it. Hermione says, "We've got to plan. We've got to figure it out!" Harry replies, "Hermione, when have any of our plans actually worked? We plan, we get there, all hell breaks loose." Have you ever felt like Harry, or are you more of a Hermione? Maybe you feel like your plans never work out like Harry, or you are like Hermione and just want to plan and plan and maybe not take decisive action. Which one is right or wrong? I would say both are.

If you desire something more in your life, you need to create a plan to get it, but don't give up when the plan doesn't work out the way you thought. Instead, you need to adjust your plan. The key is not just to create a plan but also to take action and never stop moving towards that goal or desire you want.

There are two things I like to mention about organizing your plan. First off, you don't need to do it all yourself. Find your tribe or your mastermind, if you will. Napoleon Hill talks a lot about masterminds in his book "*Think and Grow Rich*." Why does he talk about them so much? Because they are effective. Even if you only have a small group of people to help you brainstorm your plan or to help you find resources to achieve your plan, it is worth it. Two or more brains are always better than just one. We often have a vision of how things are supposed to be that we can't see clearly, and others' perspectives can help create clarity. So, surround yourself with people who can support you and help you create and activate your plan.

The next thing about planning is that you don't have to reinvent the wheel. Others have probably done what you want to do, find those people and model your plan after what they did. If you have ever seen how a pack of wolves pushes through deep snow, they all go in a line behind the lead wolf, who cuts a path in the snow for the others. The lead wolf has the hardest job and often needs to be the strongest to create that path. The other wolves follow his path. You don't have to create your own path. Success leaves clues, and if we follow those clues, we can find success as well, just by learning from those who have already done what we want to achieve.

Now I want to touch on taking action once you have the plan. It will more than likely be a mess at first. Change is always messy at first but beautiful in the end if you keep the course. If the plan you create doesn't work at first, take a pointer from the US Marines playbook: adapt, improvise, and overcome. Things won't always go according to plan, and they probably won't go at all like you first thought but keep going. Adjust as you go, make corrections as you keep working, and never give up.

There was a time in my life that was very hard, and I got depressed. I felt like a failure and almost gave up on myself. But, thanks to some amazing experiences, I decided to keep fighting and pushing forward. It was not long after I went through that point when my wife and I were at a store and saw this big rustic-looking sign that had three words on it, "Never Give Up." I told my wife I had to have that sign, we bought it, and it now hangs over our front door to remind myself and my kids never to give up and keep pushing even when things look hard or don't work out.

I remember hearing once that there is never a person who keeps pushing and striving for success who doesn't eventually find it. It's not magic; it takes effort, resilience, and creative, organized planning to reach the desires of your heart and achieve amazing success.

So, create your plan, work on it, and never give up.

~ Adam Platt

LACEY & ADAM PLATT

About Lacey Platt: Lacey is an energetic, fun loving, super mom of five! She is an Achievement Coach, Speaker and new Bestselling Author who enjoys helping everyone she can by getting to know what their needs are and then loving on them in every way that she can. Her ripple effect and impact has touched the lives of so many and continues to reach more lives every single day. Allow Lacey to help you achieve your goals with proven techniques she has created and perfected over years of coaching. Lacey and her husband have built an amazing coaching business called Arise to Connect serving people all around the world.

About Adam Platt: Adam is an Achievement Coach, Speaker, Trainer, Podcast Host and now a Bestselling Author. Adam loves to help people overcome the things stopping them from having the life they really want. Adam owns and operates Arise to Connect. Adam believes that connection with yourself, others, and your higher power are the keys to achievement and greater success in life. He is impacting thousands of people's lives with his message and coaching. He lives in Utah with his wife, five daughters, and their dog, Max.

Author's Website: *www.AriseToConnect.com*
Book Series Website & Author's Bio: *www.The13StepstoRiches.com*

Louisa Jovanovich

STOP THROWING SPAGHETTI AT THE WALL!

I'm so grateful and proud of how much I have accomplished in my life, but I have to say that most of it has been like "throwing spaghetti at the wall." I love pasta, and I was always told that you know when it's ready to eat when you pick a strand out of the pot and throw it against the wall. If it sticks, then we know it's ready. I have used the same philosophy in my life, or I used to.

While I had huge visions and goals as to what I desired, if I'm being honest, it didn't happen due to strategic planning. I have had limiting beliefs about my abilities in planning, which led me to wishful thinking that everything would just turn out the way it was supposed to.

Have you ever felt like you would start swimming with such high hopes and possibilities only to end up in the middle of the pool treading water, having to swim back to the shallow end where it was familiar and safe?

That was me!

Many people stay stuck because they are not ready or willing to learn the skills necessary to be a great swimmer. It seemed to me that saying that I don't know how to swim kept me out of the deep end with all the other amazing swimmers. It wasn't until I shifted my mindset that things started happening. So why did I keep ending up in the middle of the pool treading water? What skill sets did I need to learn to get past the hump?

That was the moment things started changing for me.

Awareness has been the most important breakthrough in my life. I accomplished this by taking inventory and getting very clear on my life and my role in my life. I am the source of exactly what I am manifesting. Although there are still ups and downs on the road, and sometimes I find myself right back in that pool, pretending I don't know how to swim, I look back at everything I have accomplished. In a way, which propels me forward so I can take action instead of living a life throwing spaghetti on the wall.

I have two children to raise who are watching my every move. I want them to see both the struggles and the successes that come from learning, growing, and believing in their self-worth. I GET to create the change I want to see for myself and my family. I GET to be responsible. I GET to create plans and execute them.

All of this realization brings me so much joy!

When you change your mindset so you are more aware, life has a way of showing us the next steps.

I want you to know that there are times when FEAR creeps in and starts filling my head with doubt. It makes me think that maybe I would be better off playing it safe, so I don't have to go out of my comfort zone. That life does NOT excite me! Not to mention it would be a false sense of security.

Napoleon Hill mentions that the first step in organized planning is aligning yourself with a group of people who will help put your plan in place and keep you accountable. These people help you generate tools on how to SHIFT so as not to go down the rabbit hole into the cavern of fear and regret. Without that support system in my life, I wouldn't have been able to stand in my power, accept mistakes that I made, and move forward without internalizing them. We all get to hold each other high as we grow. It's not always comfortable, but it is remarkable.

I have had a wonderful opportunity to put together a program right now that benefits so many people and has been a life-changing experience for me in the process. It has been a long time since that FEAR of not being good enough kept rearing its ugly head. Instead of letting it keep me in the shadows, I pushed through and said YES to myself and the process. Through saying YES to designing this mastermind program, I have been able to give and receive an abundance of love from everyone who is a part of it. I GET to see each individual from where they are when they begin the program to how they have grown and changed throughout our time together. This has become a support system for all of us. The guidance of the people we surround ourselves with and can be vulnerable with helps keep us on track. They are the cheerleaders sitting at the side of the pool, filling us with encouragement as we finally make it to the deep end.

The second step is making sure you meet with this group at least once or twice a week. This establishes the space for you and your group to devise and execute a plan to propel the whole group forward.

Now is the time to say YES to you! You deserve to swim with the experts.

Take each OPPORTUNITY seriously because it could change the course of your life. How you show up makes a BIG difference.

One of the most important things that have helped me on my journey is the "Major Attributes of Leadership" that Napoleon Hill speaks about in *Think and Grow Rich*. This is a good guide to help keep you on track as you continue to work on your ideas and tweak your plans in life:

Unwavering Courage

Become a "YES" person, so no matter what comes your way, you will say yes because new doors open up nine times out of ten. The more I have chosen to step into that unfamiliar territory, the more comfortable I have gotten doing something so unfamiliar and sometimes life-changing.

Self-Control

Deciding what reaction to have in every situation could change the course of your day. Find every possible hack to put in place to accomplish this for it to become a habit.

A Keen Sense of Justice

Be the person who knows right from wrong and chooses to act more on being the good and righteous person in any situation.

Definiteness of Decision

Self-trust leads to the definiteness of decision. I put mini-tasks in my day to help me accomplish this area. They could be as simple as cleaning up after yourself or making your bed every day. BE responsible for yourself.

Definiteness of Plans

This is the point where you stop throwing spaghetti against the wall. When I was doing that, I knew I did not have a definite plan, I just had a big dream, and I desired the way I wanted my life to turn out. I learned that I could actually see what has been working and what is not through specific planning. Based on measurable results, I see how far I have come and where I still need to go.

The Habit of Doing More than Paid For

Living out your dream is creating your Legacy. When you start the process, you realize it is not a dollar amount that drives you but the ability to change lives and make a difference. I GET to see the impact of my vision as it has come alive in the world.

A Pleasing Personality

I know how I have made it this far in life has been my personality. I can see people's greatness, even when they can't, which helps them feel so loved and seen.

Sympathy and Understanding

Every stage of life and what it brings is different for every one of us. Even when you don't know what they are going through, having compassion for others will help you grow into a better person.

Willingness To Assume Full Responsibility

I continue to shift my thinking daily, choosing beliefs that empower me vs. disempower me. Every single one of us is responsible for the actions in our own lives. As soon as you accept that, then you can move forward.

Cooperation

Working with others didn't always come easy for me because I thought it was giving away my power. It took me a while to realize that everyone has their strengths, and by becoming a team, you become more powerful than if you were alone.

I am collecting evidence daily that I am in the right place and going down the right path. My swimming strokes are getting stronger, and I am getting closer and closer to the deep end with confidence. With the help of my mastermind group, my vision is getting clearer, and I can feel safe in trusting the process. There is no way for us to know the future or what life has in store for us, but I am so grateful that I GET to show myself and the world the best of me each day.

LOUISA JOVANOVICH

About Louisa Jovanovich: Louisa is the founder of Connect with Source. She is a mindfulness and emotional intelligence coach. She enjoys helping others identify blind spots and create new beliefs which empower her clients to access a life they have never dreamed possible. She has completed 20 years of personal and transformational growth including Land-mark Forum, Gratitude Training, and is a Clarity Catalyst Certified trainer. She works with entrepreneurs who seek clarity and want to up-level their lives.

Her life experiences and school of hard knocks are what make her a knowledgeable and compassionate leader and enable her to help guide others through the process of looking for answers within in order to find success and breakthrough their limiting beliefs. Her unique coaching techniques help her clients see the truth behind the stories that are keeping them stuck in the reality they created.

Louisa is a single mother of two teenagers living in LA. Her love and compassion towards others are her superpowers, helping others reclaim their confidence, find their voice, and know their worth.

Author's Website: *www.ConnectWithSource.com*
Book Series Website & Author's Bio: *www.The13StepstoRiches.com*

Lynda Sunshine West

TO PLAN OR NOT TO PLAN, THAT IS THE QUESTION!

In 2015, I decided to embark on a journey that would forever change my life. Initially, I didn't have a plan in mind. All I knew was that I had a lot of fears, and they were stopping me from living my life.

You see, I grew up in a very volatile, abusive, alcoholic household, and that household caused me to be riddled with fear and become a people-pleaser. Something about that environment prevented me from following through with my plans. As a result, I became the ultimate procrastinator. I used to pride myself on being able to "rise to the occasion" when a deadline was fast approaching, i.e., this chapter of this book.

I believe that being a procrastinator is more of a habit caused by fear—The fear of success, the fear of failure, the fear of judgment, the fear of <name your fear>. When we procrastinate, we put off the inevitable or back ourselves into a corner where we cannot accomplish the task at hand. We have "failed when we don't accomplish the task at hand; we have "failed." When we have a fear of failure, failing means we actually succeed.

When I decided to break through one fear every day for an entire year in 2015 at the age of 51, I had no idea what results I would gain by embarking on that journey.

One of the greatest challenges I had throughout my life was conquering procrastination. As I started breaking through one fear every day, I started gaining more confidence in myself and started planning in my business and my personal life.

I have notepads galore. Notes about what I'm going to do today, next week, the goals of what I'm going to accomplish in the next year to five years, notebooks about people I have met along my journey, and ideas that pop up into my head. I never carried a notebook until 2015, the year that literally changed my entire life.

While everything I do does not lead to success, I become more and more organized every year. What's fascinating is that I spent 23 years working as a legal secretary (a very organized position where lack of organization will get you fired). Once I became an entrepreneur, it was as if my organizational skills were stripped from me. I still had the organizational skills, but I refused to use them because I felt constricted for 36 years in the corporate world and was in denial that those were actually great skills and I could utilize them to lead to my success. Now that I was on my own, I had to take on a different mindset and train myself how to be organized to achieve the results I wanted.

There is no straight line when it comes to organized planning. What works for me may not work for you, and what works for you may not work for the next person. One of the things my mastermind group did was to try out various techniques to become organized. Every two weeks, someone would bring a new idea to the group for us all to try. We worked on that one technique for two weeks and then reported our findings.

What was cool was that some of the ladies during this process found the organized planning tools that worked perfectly for them, while others still struggled to find that tool that worked. I found that having small notebooks that I carry around with me works well. They keep me organized, and even though sometimes it may seem that they're disorganized, my mind can track what I've written in which notebook.

The point here is to try different techniques until you find what works for you. There are so many different planners out there, and I hear a lot of people talking about how amazing some of them are and how they have shifted their lives, but when I tried them out, they simply didn't work for me.

Napoleon Hill talks about creating a plan and working that plan, and if it doesn't work, replace it with a new plan. It's really that simple. With all the business ventures I have attempted and experienced failure, I kept getting back up because I know deep down in my soul that I have a gift that will provide tremendous value to so many people. I just had to keep going until I figured out what it was. While I'm a mildly organized person, I like to have an open flow of plans. I work the openness into my organized planning, so it's easy to do when I want to shift to something different.

Please take a little bit of time to sit down and figure out what you want out of your life, write out the plan to get the result you want, and then go for it. Don't let anything stop you, especially procrastination.

LYNDA SUNSHINE WEST

About Lynda Sunshine West: Lynda is known as The Fear Buster. She's a Speaker, 10 Time Best-Selling Author, Book Publisher, Executive Film Producer, Red Carpet Interviewer, and the Founder of Women Action Takers. At age 51 she faced one fear every day for an entire year. In doing so, she gained an exorbitant amount of confidence and uses what she learned by facing a fear every day to fulfill her mission of helping 5 million women entrepreneurs gain the confidence to share their voice with the world. Her collaboration books, mastermind, podcast, and many more opportunities give women from all over the world the opportunity to share their voice with the world. She believes in cooperation and collaboration and loves connecting with like-minded people.

Author's Website: *www.ActionTakersPublishing.com*
Book Series Website & Author's Bio: *www.The13StepstoRiches.com*

Maris Segal & Ken Ashby

BEFORE YOU DO ANYTHING

We constantly remind each other, our teams, and the business clients we coach that "Before we "do" anything, there is always something else that needs to be completed first." What it takes to build and execute an organized plan of any kind, whether in our personal or professional lives, is a combination of leading with our hearts and our heads, the ultimate dynamic duo. The first part of the plan will be driven by desire and creating a "heart-centered" vision, and the second part of the plan will be more mechanical, creating the "head-centered" steps for getting it done.

So often, we find that when our executive and entrepreneurial clients come to us, they want to dive head-first into the "doing" and begin with the mechanics versus first being clear on the vision. This approach never leads to success. Baseball legend and humorist Yogi Berra once quipped, "If you don't know where you are going, you'll end up someplace else." Our experience over thirty years has proven that there is no substitute for aligning action with the vision. So, we have developed a method to support this approach to organized planning called **D.R.I.V.E. Now!**

D.R.I.V.E. Now! Focuses first on the underlying purpose, the "why," before getting into the mechanics of the "what." As executive producers, speakers, business consultants, trainers, and coaches, we've seen the impact of using this approach to build and bring a vision to life.

Using DRIVE Now involves every aspect of our lives: family, business, community, fun, health, wealth, and personal growth.

D.R.I.V.E. - Desire, Relationship, Intention, Vision, and Empowerment includes five critical steps in designing a plan. Like building a house, DRIVE Now will set a solid foundation and a supportive frame for the plan. Now! is the part of this tool that creates some urgency for laying the groundwork before taking empowered action. Why wait? Life is NOW! We invite you to explore this chapter with a lens into how you are leading your life. You may want to grab a pen and paper and follow the exercises below or come back to them at a later time.

Desire - From a place of imagination, curiosity, and discovery, this is where ideas are born. Desire offers the springboard to creating a personal/professional vision. Desire pulls the dream(s) forward into acknowledgment. Desire is a feeling from the depths of your heart and the center of your being. Desire is constructed around one question - "What do you really want?" Being unapologetic and unwaveringly clear around what we "want" gets all the cogs of the wheel working in unison. Desire has no limits. Dare to desire what's possible.

> *Exercise: Pick an area of your life, health, family, finance, work, and list any desires you have in this category, be very specific. Leave 3-4 lines in between each item.*

Relationship - Accessing your connection to all aspects of what you desire is an "inside and outside job," which begins with being in a solid relationship with yourself "inside." Your positive mindset, the voice that says, "I can, and I will," sets the tone for your success and opens the door to how you engage with others, "outside," who can help you succeed. Negative "inside" thoughts such as "I'm not good enough," or "someone else is more qualified," or "we don't have the funds" are all limiting beliefs that hold you back and will always show up in how you engage with others.

This has the potential to sabotage the success of your plan. Planning is not a lone-wolf job, and we step into our leadership by creating, reviving, or reinventing relationships that will lift our "desires" to the magic point of flow. Success often hinges on the quality of our relationships. Remember, relationships work both ways, the giving and the receiving. If my relationship to a stated goal is surrounded by limiting beliefs, then my leadership in accomplishing the desire will be ineffective. Being in positive, strong relationships with ourselves and our desires provides a powerful basis to create a superior experience.

Exercise: For each "desire" listed above, consider two types of connections that will support bringing this desire to life. First, the people in your life who are authentically there for you as you navigate change and growth, those whose radical honesty and expertise you trust. Secondly, the people who have the professional expertise and knowledge that you may not possess. Under each desire, list the person or type of expertise you will need. Now match the people and the role you see them playing. Of course, you won't have all the answers, and that's OK.

Intention - Having a desire is wistful without the intention to follow through. The intention is the commitment to what we plan to create. Wavering only proves that you are not yet fully committed. Sometimes it takes being uncomfortable and breaking through fears, which are important growth steps. The intention is the determination that supports the "I can, and I will" to ensure meeting the outcome. It is easy to get distracted from intention when focusing on the mechanics, the "doing." Being committed to an intention promotes a willingness and responsibility to all involved to keep moving forward regardless of challenges that may unexpectedly pop up to block our way. Intention is the umbrella over all plans and expectations that helps us stand firm, believing that anything is possible.

Exercise: On your paper create a section that says "Intention." Now look at your "desire" list and complete this sentence, "I am committed to (what) _____ by (when) _____."

Vision – Vision at work or home is born from "desire," and vision is the big picture perspective of what you believe to be possible. You can see it and live it as if it has already happened. A clear, concise vision is not only the key to accomplishing our goals but also the linchpin for enrolling the support of a team. After outlining our Desire and Intention, we literally experience the Vision, and then we put it to paper in a statement. Vision, when shared, is the tool that creates a picture of completion. It evokes emotion and inspires family, staff, investors, and clients to engage their resources and partner with you to bring your vision to fruition. We have worked with Fortune 500 companies, entrepreneurs, and not-for-profits that were launched with a powerful vision, and they succeed when the entire organization is connected and invested. Unfortunately, we have also seen great visions unfulfilled when leadership transitioned, and the vision was not passed on and integrated throughout the organization. In business or at home, an organized plan incorporates connections and strengths and illuminates weaknesses. Purpose-driven teams and families who are aligned with a vision, and have the opportunity to be heard, feel valued, and are committed to collective success. Olympians are a great example! They have a clear vision; that they will be standing on the podium, representing their country, and winning a medal. They live it, breathe it, engage others, and believe it every day, even when things get tough.

Exercise: Can you begin to see your desires aligned with a Big Vision? Write a statement that encompasses what you "see" one year down the road. Imagine sitting with a friend you have not seen in a year. What are you telling them about your life, be very specific about all details; how do you feel when telling them? Now write what you see, and don't worry about getting it "perfect," it's your vision.

Empowerment – This step is where we detail the "getting it done" mechanics for each stage of bringing our vision to life! From this point, we engage ourselves and others to take "empowered action." Here we answer the question; "What detailed steps are required to fulfill our vision by the date we set?" There is no room for emotion in this step, and this is where we set milestones and acknowledge every success along the way. Small wins build big momentum! Although we may have a plan, things happen, and change, which is inevitable, this can cause frustration and resistance in ourselves and the team/family. So, equally important is setting evaluation milestones to address the changes when conditions and circumstances shift. Think of the shift that the Covid- 19 pandemic caused for us all. *Forbes* magazine tells us that one of the major reasons that strategy fails is because of "an unwillingness or inability to change." We've learned that being in relationship to this change is part of the empowered action process. Resisting change can slow down, if not completely halt, the best-made plans because most people want to stay close to their comfort zone. Change challenges "comfort zones" and offers an opportunity to reframe a situation and see it from another possibility. When we are nimble and adapt, empowered action supports breaking through change. By encouraging empowered action in our own lives, and the work of those around us, we can soar together to new levels of leadership.

> *Exercise: Under your vision statement, list the steps it will take to get there and what support you will seek. Once this is complete, you can begin to add "by when" dates.*

Remember that organized planning takes patience and time, and a leader is cognizant of both! Time is constant; our relationship to time is a choice.

We hope that DRIVE Now! will come in handy as you plan your work and work your plan. Great leaders have a plan which includes purpose, people, and process, all working in partnership! So here's to you creating your Organized Plan. Plan it, live it, love it, own it, and enjoy all the possibilities that may open up!

MARIS SEGAL
& KEN ASHBY

About Maris Segal and Ken Ashby: From Mindset to Marketing, Ken Ashby & Maris Segal, a husband and wife dynamic duo, have spent the last thirty-plus years bringing an innovative, collaborative voice to issues, causes, and brands. As entrepreneurs, activists, business strategists, executive producers, coaches, authors, speakers, and trainers, Ken & Maris work with the public and private sectors from boardrooms and classrooms to the world stage. They are known for creating high touch experiences that unite diverse populations across a broad spectrum of business, policy, and social issues.

Their leadership expertise in Business Relationship Marketing, Organizational Change & Cultural Inclusion, Personal Growth, Project Management, Public Affairs, and Philanthropy Strategies has been called upon by companies and their agencies. Their experience includes: consumer and financial brands, Olympic organizers, Super Bowls, America's 400th Anniversary, Harvard Kennedy School, Archdiocese of LA and NY Papal visit planners, the White House and celebrities across the arts, entertainment, sports, and culinary genres.

With Ken's expertise as an award-winning singer-songwriter, they launched ONE SONG, a songwriting workshop series designed to unleash creativity in individuals and teams.

Their **DRIVE** method: **D**esire, **R**elationships, **I**ntention, **V**ision and **E**mpowerment sits at the core of their companies Prosody Creative Services, ONE SONG, and Segal Leadership Global to set a path for every client to Build High Performing Businesses & Elevate Personal & Professional Leadership for Maximum Impact & a 360-degree Thriving Life!

Author's Website: *www.ProsodyCreativeServices.com*
Book Series Website & Author's Bio: *www.The13StepstoRiches.com*

Mel Mason

MAKING INSPIRED ORDER OUT OF ASPIRATIONAL CHAOS

Venus and Serena Williams' father had a mantra: "If you fail to plan, you plan to fail." He lived this creed and made his five daughters do the same. This often involved two-hour family meetings where they would strategically plan their next moves. I'm not just talking about routine plans like tomorrow Venus will practice tennis. No, these were in-depth plans, complete with back-ups. What time will the girls practice? What specifically are they working on tomorrow? Where will they practice? What happens if it rains?

When Richard Williams asked his daughters, "Did you write down your plan?" he wasn't looking for a sentence; he was looking for a multi-page analysis. Long-term plans were discussed, too, outlining his daughters' career trajectories. This in-depth planning proved to be successful as Venus and Serena went on to earn global GOAT ("Greatest of All Time") status, with 30 Grand Slam singles titles and eight Olympic gold medals between them.

I'm not saying that this mantra was solely responsible for the Williams sisters' success. Rigorous training, natural athletic prowess, and admirable integrity on and off the court made Venus and Serena the stars they are today. But even Serena has attributed much of her success to the values instilled in her by her father: "It's only now that I see the real value of learning how to plan and organize my thoughts. Now I understand how important those lessons were and what part they played in my life." Sure, they still would've been incredible tennis players without the plan, but would anyone have known it?

What I'm getting to here is my favorite kind of planning: Organizational. Come on: I'm The Clutter Expert! Of course, having a plan is key, but what we don't talk about enough is how important it is that even your plan has to be organized.

Organizational Planning is the process of defining a company's reason for existing, setting goals aimed at realizing full potential, and creating increasingly discrete tasks to meet those goals. To put it simply, organizational planning is Your Main Plan, organized into smaller, more easily manageable pieces. It's a way of making it all make sense in your brain and then creating actionable, progressive steps.

Organizational planning is typically broken down into four categories: **Strategic, Tactical, Operational,** and **Contingency.** The idea is that each category leads to the next, a clear and beautiful process that can be repeated as often as necessary.

Strategic planning is where you flesh out the big picture. Long-term goals, dreams, and overall vision for your idea all go into this planning phase. You can do this in varying increments of time— one year, five years, ten years, etc. Specificity will take you far, my friend. Although, I wouldn't go smaller than one year because that's becoming very tactical.

Tactical planning gets a little more intense. This is where you decide how to make the Strategic plan happen. If you have a five-year strategic plan, you'll need several smaller plans that get you to that five-year goal. For instance, if you want to be a best-selling author in five years, you'll need to find a publisher sometime before the five years are up. Sometime before that, you'll need to do some writing. Sometime before that, you'll need to have an idea for a book. Do you get where we're going with this?

Reverse engineer your big picture goal. What tiny goals fill in the large gap between where you are now and where you want to be?

This brings us to **Operational** planning—which might be my favorite. This is the breakdown of your tactical planning. To reach your short-term goals, what does your day-to-day need to look like? This is where you decide what you need to accomplish each day and how you plan to accomplish it. You must be intentional here. For example, if one of your small goals is to have a new client by the end of the month, that means that on the first of the month, you better start fishing. You can't wait until the last week of the month to find a new client—you'll inevitably miss your deadline. If a small-term deadline gets pushed, then so does the next one. If this continues, your five-year plan becomes a ten-year plan before you know it. Of course, curveballs will be thrown. This is why it's so important to manage your day-to-day. As best you can, prevent any sidebars. But when you can't, at least you'll have your Contingency Plan.

Contingency planning is the work you prepare for but hope you never have to utilize. This is "in case of emergency" planning. You tell yourself it won't come to this, but it might, and if it does, you'll be glad you made a plan. No one likes to think about worst-case scenarios, but a backup plan could be the difference between momentary derailment or permanent decommission.

I wish I could say that I did this all right the first time. But unfortunately, I learned the hard way, leaning heavily on contingency planning.

When I came up with my business idea (during my Hoarders-Eureka moment), I dove right in without any sort of plan. I just thought, "Oh, I'll start this business!" I bought one book and supplies and launched my business in January 2014. I didn't think much about anything other than the product. I spend an inappropriate amount of time focusing on a lubricant for sticky drawers in clients' homes, thinking it would be a hugely important factor. It wasn't.

I was so passionate about my offering and focused on how to execute it that I didn't think about anything else. By February of 2014, I realized, "Oh crap, I kinda need some clients."

Shortly after, the universe offered me—via Facebook—a free ticket to a local event for business owners about how to build a list of clients. I went, thinking, "Oh yes, see? Everything is working out!" And for a while, things did seem to work. I met the woman who became my business coach for the next few years at the event. I attended her masterclass workshop on building an online database of subscribers. Finally, I felt like I was on the right track.

With much enthusiasm, I jumped right into another mastermind program, thinking this train would just keep building momentum. As it turned out, I wasn't ready, and in trying to force my dream without a plan, I skipped over a lot of valuable information I still very much needed. My business floundered, and I racked up a ton of debt. I had to step away.

With no real contingency plan, I was back working for someone else. My business was a decommissioned train collecting rust.

Back in the "real world," I had time to consider what went wrong. I looked at it from every angle and quickly realized that I went into this whole thing without any organized sort of plan. Me! The self-proclaimed Clutter Expert hadn't thought to organize her own business. So I decided that I would try again once I got my life in order. But this time, I'd do some organizational planning.

In 2018, I re-launched. Strategically, I knew I wanted to end up coaching clients through their clutter. But tactically, I knew I needed to gain notoriety and expertise by physically de-cluttering clients' spaces. Operationally, that meant I needed to get involved, build relationships, and find clients. My day-to-day life became all about networking.

I wasted no time getting on the right track with a multi-faceted plan. I joined the local Chamber of Commerce and went to every event.

Constant networking was not super fun for me—I consider myself super introverted—but I made it my priority. I attended so many meetings and events that the community joke became, "Mel is Everywhere." I was everywhere, and it worked. In less than ten months, I'd generated $19K just from my Chamber connections alone. The train was picking up speed.

When Covid-19 hit, I had to resort to my contingency plan: moving my business entirely online, remotely coaching clients through their clutter. But the funny thing is that my contingency plan was actually my long-term strategic goal. This shift put me exactly where I wanted to be, years before I thought I'd be there. But without the plan, who knows if my business would've been primed to take advantage of such an opportunity.

Organizational planning works if you work at it. The key is in the willingness to return to the drawing board, time and time again. With a plan, failure isn't necessarily the end of the line; it's just a pivot. Unfortunately, lack of persistence is ultimately why most people don't make it. For example, when inventing the lightbulb, Thomas Edison failed 9,999 times before getting it right. Another way to look at it? Thomas Edison had 9,999 contingency plans.

Organize your plan. Get input from a mentor you trust, and then use your skills and wisdom to see it through. Keep what works; throw out what doesn't. The best thing about organizational planning is that it's cyclical; the plan grows, evolves, and continues. The dream only ends when you say it ends.

MEL MASON

About Mel Mason: International Best-Selling Author Mel Mason is The Clutter Expert, and as a sexual abuse survivor, she grew up depressed, suicidal, and surrounded by clutter. What she realized after coming back from the brink of despair and getting through her own chaos was that the outside is just a mirror of the inside, and if you only address the outside without changing the inside, the clutter keeps coming back.

That set her on a mission to empower people around the world to get free from clutter inside and out, so they can experience happiness and abundance in every area of their lives.

She is the author of *Freedom from Clutter: The Guaranteed, Foolproof, Step-by-Step Process to Remove the Stuff That's Weighing You Down*

Author's website: *www.FreeGiftFromMel.com*
Book Series Website & Author's Bio: *www.The13StepsToRiches.com*

Dr. Miatta Hampton

SUCCESS BLUEPRINT

A plan not written down is a plan to waste time. To achieve greatness and success, you must have a plan. If you want to live a life of excellence, you have to come out of mediocrity. Come out of average and plan for an amazing life. Having an organized plan speaks to your success and the abundance you are expecting to flood your life. You have decided that now is the time to level up in life and business. You are turning your thoughts, dreams, and vision into reality—goal setting and creating tasks to achieve those goals. You have waited long enough. Today is the day you will choose to formulate a plan or rework your plan and pivot to success. You are on your way to writing that book, starting the business, getting those coaching clients, and finishing that degree. You just need a success blueprint and the self-discipline to execute daily.

There I was, a ball of emotions, irritated, annoyed, tearful. I couldn't put my finger on exactly what I was feeling. I sat and attempted to get in touch with my feeling, get in touch with my emotions. "What emotion are you feeling?' I asked myself. Unorganized and unmotivated were the answers that popped into my head. Why? Because I didn't plan. Why? Because I was tired. Why? Because I was working a 9 to 5 and building a business simultaneously. Why? Because my 9 to 5 was financing my business. Why? Because I hadn't generated enough money in my business. And I realized that the plan that I currently had was not working. I was working on the business instead of working in the business. I felt like I was going nowhere fast. I was moving in circles. I had everything that I needed to succeed, yet I was not seeing the true works of my hands. I was not generating my ideal revenue; I was not attracting my ideal coaching client. I had set goals and written the plan, but I still did not see the desired results. Something was missing. Were my goals specific enough? Were they measurable, achievable, realistic, and time-oriented? I was ready to quit and give up, but I knew that the only guarantee I had if I quit was that I would never see my dreams come to fruition. So, I took a deep breath, wiped the tears from my eyes, stood in front of the mirror, and recited my affirmation.

"God's abundance is operating in my life. It floods my life with no hesitation, and immediately all my needs, goals, and desires are met through endless wisdom, knowledge, and strategy. I will grow in wisdom in business, strategies, and stature and in favor with God and man because I believe all things are possible with God. I will be anxious for nothing. I will set my mind on whatever things are good, honest, lovely, just, trustworthy, and if there be any virtue, I will think on these things. Good things are happening for and to me in my personal life and in business. I have the influence; I have the creativity, I have the network, I have the strategy."

I devised a plan to attract my ideal client and wrote down my market breakdown and how I would get coaching clients. First, I had to look for the opportunities in business, and it would start with understanding what barriers I had in my way, creating my market breakdown, and identifying my ideal client. As an entrepreneur, coach, speaker, or author, maybe there are barriers prohibiting you from getting to the next level, generating the type of income you desire, landing that next speaking gig, or writing that book. Maybe you start and stop, or you are just flat-out indecisive. With that being said, I have identified the top three reasons why some people struggle to find success: procrastination, fear, and being indecisive.

Procrastination

You are delaying putting in the work to get to the next level. Success doesn't come easy, and it doesn't come overnight. It comes by putting one foot in front of the other, doing the necessary work to achieve greatness, and believing in yourself and your ability to make things happen. When you are procrastinating, you are simply trying to avoid feelings of stress, overwhelm, and anxiety.

Fear

You are afraid to go to the next level, questioning whether you have what it takes to generate a million dollars in revenue. Fear will keep you stagnant and keep you from showing up for your tribe, your audience, your prospects, and your ideal client. When fear appears to rule the day, affirm who you are and those gifts and talents you have inside of you. Repeat this to yourself out loud: I am the best keep secret. My gifts and talents set me apart from everyone else. I am executing with confidence.

Indecisive

Your inability to decide will cause you to miss opportunities that can catapult you and your business to the next level. Decide that you are going to go all in. Decide that you are smart enough. Decide that you have everything that you need to succeed. Decide you are worth it. Decide to pivot to success. When you learn to conquer procrastination, fear, and indecisiveness, you will unleash the greatness you have inside you. Once you eliminate those self-limiting beliefs, you will find your own secret formula to success and devise an organized plan to change your life trajectory. Once you do that, you can focus on your marketing breakdown, getting those coaching clients, and creating your own goals strategy for creating an organized plan.

You must commit to doing three things to come up with your own success blueprint. First, write it down; the plan or the vision starts with the desire you have in your heart. Write down your plan, and you are on your way to success. Studies suggest that people who write down their vision and how they plan to execute their vision are 82% more successful than people who don't take the time to get their plans on paper. You must write the vision and make it plain. Second, be decisive. Decide to increase your efforts. Don't waste time deliberating on your future. Instead, go after what you want, and pursue it with passion. Lastly, practice self-discipline. There will be days when you may feel like giving up, when you feel like your back is against the wall, and when you will feel unmotivated; that's when self-discipline kicks in. Put self-gratification on the back burner and push toward your goals. It's go-time. Perform your market breakdown. Take some time and answer the following question:

Who is your ideal client? Where do they live?
What are their likes & dislikes?
What are their gender and age?
How much money do they make?
Why do you think they want to work with you?

DR. MIATTA HAMPTON

About Dr. Miatta Hampton: Dr. Miatta Hampton is a nurse leader, #1 best-selling author, speaker, coach, and minister. Miatta impacts others with her powerful, relatable messages of pursing purpose, and she empowers her audiences to live life on purpose and according to their dreams. She coaches and inspires women to turn chaos into cozy, pivot to success, and how to profit in adversity. Miatta provides tools and resources for personal, professional, and financial growth.

Author's website: *www.DrMiattaSpeaks.com*
Book Series Website & Author's Bio: *www.The13StepsToRiches.com*

Michael D. Butler

THE PERSEPCTIVE OF DISORGANIZED PLANNING

In order to understand Organized Planning, we must first look at it from the other angle; yes, from the angle of disorganization.

The ability to be organized and micro-focused means we first had to take a 30,000-foot view of the situation project or proposal macro-focused.

This is where the saying, "You can't see the forest for all of the trees," comes from. If we're too laser-focused on the minute details, we can easily forget the "why" we do it. And "why" is a mighty driver for corporate culture, passion, motivation, and determination that helps us finish a project.

A person that looks disorganized could actually be very organized in their brain. Since they look at things differently, they don't follow the status quo; they break the rules and appear to be a maverick. They must first demolish the status quo and the norms to uncover the infrastructure and rebuild it. They ask probing questions and make people nervous; they are the disruptors. Love them or hate them, they are the early adopters who take the greatest risk, normally suffer the most collateral damage but reap the greatest rewards as they lead the pack to new ways of thinking and doing things.

They're the ones who zig when everyone else is zagging. They are the risk-takers. They didn't believe the world was flat. They were ostracized, persecuted, made fun of and marginalized, and later celebrated as heroes.

The world needs organized planning. These are the engineers, architects, civil engineers, landscapers, and plumbers. But the world also needs dreamers, creatives, artists, and inventors. Those who think outside the box. Those who dream. Those who ask "why" and "why not" and keep asking questions, keep exploring. They are always looking for a better way to build and deliver the same widget.

Not all disarray is disorganization. For projects to get completed properly in any industry or endeavor, the raw materials must be properly staged and inventoried to create a strategic plan and executive summary of how the operations and fulfillment will flow in our new enterprise. This needs to be staffed properly and sequentially for the work to flow and the desired completion date to be met.

You can take the fast route, the scenic route, or create a new route. Organized planners are good at implementation, but they would do well to work with the pioneers, innovators, and idea generators to find the quickest, most efficient, and most profitable route to the finish line. The upside to organized planning is that it's systematized and predictable; the downside is that systems can fail, and you need a backup plan when they do.

Last summer I was speaking in Brighton, England, at a conference. I had rented a car because I would be in England for ten days and wanted to get used to driving on the other side of the road. Since I'm from the US, it would be quite different for me; not only that but most of the rental cars in Europe are standard transmissions and not automatic. I grew up driving a standard with a stick shift in high school, so that was fun, but driving on the British side of the street did take some getting used to.

Driving through Manchester to Liverpool at 5 pm during rush hour traffic, my GPS quit working. It was raining with heavy cloud cover, so I could not determine the direction from the sun. So I actually had to stop and ask for directions and, specifically, which way was north. It's not that

I was disorganized; I was very organized about my trip to Liverpool to see my grandson. But my system, the GPS, failed me, and I had to depend on a backup system, asking for directions.

History is filled with inspiring stories about amazing plans that had to be re-evaluated because the plans changed in mid-stream. Christopher Columbus thought he had sailed around the world when he found the West Indies, only to discover that he had discovered The Americas.

How many West Indies were discovered because your ship was blown off course, and you thought you were in India? Don't get frustrated if your plan goes crazy; just remember you may discover something revolutionary that will positively impact the world. Don't assign shame or blame if things don't go as planned. Simply rework your plan, adapt, change, be nimble, reassess and keep moving forward.

I made it to Liverpool that day and spent some great time with my grandson, but I had to depend on an alternate plan to arrive quickly and safely.

Get organized and be prepared for the unseen and unanticipated by looking at things from another angle. Take the macro view to see how all your organized planning and process work together. Be sure they flow together sequentially. Don't be afraid to move some processes or people around to optimize for maximum outcome.

MICHAEL D. BUTLER

About Michael D. Butler: As a global book publisher and speaker Butler is a recognized authority in the book publishing space. Helping authors and speakers evolve and create platforms of influence in an ever-changing marketplace.

The CEO of The Mark Victor Hansen Library with over 80 New York Times Bestselling titles, global distribution and sales with over half a billion books sold.

Founder at BeyondPublishing.net his authors have spoken in fitty countries and on six continents. He's most proud of his four grown sons and two grandsons.

Author's Website: *www.MichaelDButler.com*
Book Series Website & Author's Bio: *www.The13StepsToRiches.com*

Michelle Cameron Coulter & Al Coulter

THE GIFT OF PLANNING

"Tell me what you plan to do with your one wild and precious life?"
~ Mary Oliver

I know the value of organized planning.

We do organized planning as Olympians training for the Olympics. It takes a team, an organized plan with quadrennial planning, bringing the best of the best together and brainstorming what is needed, who is needed, taking care of everyone, and the big picture of the vision and goal—to reach the podium, to be our absolute best.

These past two years have been challenging for everyone in so many ways. Creating forward momentum to a vision has been tested.

The most challenging has been even knowing where to start in these last few months, which for me has come from losing my mom to COVID.

She was a strong, vibrant, and incredible woman who knew how to constantly create and find a way and get BIG things done, including raising a blended family of 10 kids. She was a brilliant, resourceful entrepreneur. She would have a vision and find a way and the resources, even launching her last company at 75 years young, so many of the lessons and traits of planning come into play, along with vision, faith, desire, and trust.

I found myself having my knees taken out from under me, asking the big question. In the end, what really matters? What is the legacy I want to leave?

I had to get my feet back under me and make a plan. We all have one life to live full-on, with no regrets.

To create the plan—the big vision—we need to be aware of the impact and the people and gifts we are bringing to the table to source and support each other in something bigger than any of us can do alone.

I got to revisit when I was most on purpose and fully stepped into that vision and plan again. It was a plan to touch millions of lives and encourage them to play full-on to their ultimate potential and leave nothing on the table. It's the kind of plan that squeezes out every little gift of potential and impact we can all create.

Throughout this plan, we need to be aware of the things that can pull us away when not fully conscious and on purpose and aware of what is possible.

We all have Gold Medal potential in so many areas of our lives.

When everything is said and done, what legacy do we want to leave behind? Who do we want to BE in the process?

What are our greatest gifts that we get to embrace and not waste entirely?

It's time to stop waiting and trying to figure it out ourselves or to do it independently.

We all have such a beautiful, powerful, and extraordinary potential to be fully lived and experienced when we create that plan and vision with faith, desire, trust, and an organized plan. The sum of all parts is greater than the varying parts every single time.

Perhaps one of the difficulties of creating an organized plan comes when we don't have a clear vision or feel lost.

I have found that having the faith to move forward and create momentum will begin to take shape, and clarity will come.

An organized plan is a starting place that will be moving and constantly evolving–especially as we grow and continue to evolve ourselves.

A plan is something that gets to be a guiding light that will shine and attract brilliance as it gets clearer and clearer, stronger and stronger.

The gift of planning is a constant and never-ending improvement system. Our plans grow as our success and potential grows.

I received a tiny little trophy for the most improved swimmer in my second year of swimming. I was awful when I started; I was shy, quiet, and a sickly little kid. I cherished this little trophy because it made me realize what is possible for me. Somebody saw something in me that I didn't yet see.

As athletes, we set our vision for the **Big Goal.** Then we would break it down and reverse-engineer it into chunks; annual, quarterly, monthly, weeks, days, and hourly. It is built on a strong foundation of the basics and continues from there.

A big part of planning is the ability to organize what needs to be done and when. It contains what strength and expertise needs to be brought around the table to form the powerhouse team – to achieve the vision outcome – what time is needed.

If we don't plan, we are planning to fail or leave everything up to chance.

Jim Rohn said it best, "If you don't plan, you will fall into someone else's plan, and they don't have much planned for you."

The power of **Review Revise:** Where are we? Are we on track? What is working and what is not? A great example of getting feedback was not only the huge value of constant feedback from our coaches to see what we couldn't see; we also had the use of videos at our practices.

As synchronized swimmers, you can't actually see what you're doing. We would work on the part of our routine and video it. We would then watch and analyze the video. What are we doing well, and what needs to adjust? What would we have missed if we hadn't stopped watching that video and made corrections? We found things we would not have known, which helped us excel faster and more efficiently.

Is what you are doing taking you closer to what you want to achieve or are you busy being busy spinning your wheels?

The Power of Feedback

Planning, evaluation, revising, and persevering never really stop.

We have the opportunity to crystalize desire into action through an Optimized Plan, as Hill stated in *Think and Grow Rich.*

After my swimming career, the last thing I wanted was to schedule or make a plan. My life had been planned right down to the minute, every detail, what I ate, and drank, how much I slept, my heart rate, and what I was doing daily, weekly, and monthly. So the last thing I wanted was structure.

It took me a while to realize the massive power of a plan and having some structure. I have also seen the power of having flexibility in the plan now.

Be aware of and identify the gap between where you are and where you want to go, and then create a plan.

Consistently review and revise your plan. Work closer to the goal and vision during each renewal period.

We get clarity when we take action and see what is working and what needs to be adjusted.

Having outside input is incredibly valuable because sometimes we cannot see what we cannot see (the proverbial "forest for the trees"). We get to be open to possibilities outside. Having other experts with similar values understand the vision that can support us in the blind spots can help us expedite the process and elevate the quality.

Another huge thing about a plan is that if we don't have one or make a conscious effort to create a plan, time flies and continues to go by fast, and we find ourselves in the same place again—still with no progress.

Time will tick, so making a plan with intention is critical to actualizing the goal or vision. It sounds so simple; it's easy to do and easy not to do.

For example, in our relationship, having a goal and intention to be closer, more connected in communication, and improve the quality of the relationship, does not just happen by going through the motions. We have found the importance of planning non-negotiable weekly dates. We know it's a great idea, and we can have all the intentions to spend more quality time; we also have 100% gone for weeks without having had a date. It's easy to become complacent and time keeps on flying unless we plan and create a non-negotiable scheduled time and commit to it.

Relationships don't pull apart overnight. We get to create a plan together, or it won't happen. It is easy to be complacent, lazy-dazy about scheduling the time and organizing plans with our schedules, non-negotiable commitment to ourselves, not leaving it up to chance.

This is true in every area of our lives. If we don't have clear intentions and make a plan, it's easy for the days, months, or years to fly by, and we wonder what happened. We need to create and schedule non-negotiable commitments, plan time for our health, relationships, business, family, financial achievements, and goals, and then schedule those other things into our plan.

Stop and take a moment. What do we want to create? How do we want to design our lives? Then make that plan and allocate the time and resources to the commitment's energy.

Then check in with the plan. There is no failure, only feedback. Is the plan working? Are my actions taken closer to our vision or further away? What needs to adjust? What support do we need? How can we approach this differently? What do we get to celebrate what we are achieving? Celebrating or growth and wins actually builds on our momentum and Joy/Enjoy Factor!

Life is really "expect the unexpected." But don't let that stop us from making a plan. We get to adjust as we go yet still move forward, have fun and create the lives we want. Putting an actual plan in place is an instrumental part of that.

So giddy up – here we go. What do you want to create? Design your life and make it happen. The gift of planning – it's Go-time - Life is Now!

MICHELLE CAMERON COULTER & AL COULTER

About Michelle Cameron Coulter: Michelle is an Olympic gold medalist, entrepreneur, mother of four, community leader raising millions of dollars for charities, global inspirational leader, and founder and CEO of Inspiring Possibilities.

About Al Coulter: Al is a two-time Olympian in volleyball, captain of Team Canada, world record holder in matches representing one's country in any sport, with over 735 matches, entrepreneur, father of four, and personal best coach, specializing in relationships, team, and resilience.

Michelle and Al are the embodiment of today's leaders. Strong and empowering, they embraced life's challenges with strength and courage. They bring insight, compassion, depth, and inspiration to the table with multiple world championships, three Olympics, an Olympic gold medal, marriage, and four children.

They are sought-after inspirational leaders. Through their speaking, workshops, and retreats, their gift and passion is to inspire possibilities and support people to embrace their greatness in a real, authentic, healthy, and vibrant way—creating thriving community, connection, and one's own gold medal results.

Author's website: *www.MichelleCameronCoulter.com*
Book Series Website & Author's Bio: *www.The13StepsToRiches.com*

Michelle Mras

WIND BENEATH YOUR WINGS

"The universe doesn't give you what you ask for with your thoughts; it gives you what you demand with your actions. In essence, you don't get what you want; you get what you are."
~ Steve Maraboli

It is important to surround yourself with others that have strengths that you lack and whom you work harmoniously with. This group must consist of people who believe that defeat is not the end.

So far, we've acquired vastly diverse perspectives from the authors who have contributed to the prior volumes of the *13 Steps to Riches* series. Although we read the same material, the insight we gain is based on our past experiences and how we interpreted the lessons. As a result, the meaning reveals itself differently to each reader.

Regardless of which author(s) you resonate with, there comes time to initiate, plan and make your desire play out through faith, auto-suggestion, specialized knowledge, and igniting the desire into action with imagination.

What will you do now? Are you a leader or a follower? I suggest that it is time to be both. A leader of self while simultaneously being a follower of stronger leaders. We need to swing between leader and follower to reach the next level.

It's time to make a plan. Throughout the process of learning the steps in *Think and Grow Rich*, it is clear that no one is in the wealth game alone. We need to gather a group of individuals around us to achieve continually. This group of similar yet not-like-minded minds will have mastered different aspects of the process as well as those able to imagine what can be.

This mastermind of individuals must also have a can-do attitude. They are individuals that see failures as lessons to rebuild and circumvent, not cave to. We need this mindset to help each other grow past our own limiting beliefs.

Organized planning is a skill that develops out of desperate necessity. During my college days, I remember I was in a very difficult class, Differential Equations. Engineering students lovingly called it DiffyQs. That class was the bane of my existence. There were mathematical constructs that I simply couldn't grasp. I was failing the class. A few fellow students and I decided that joining our thoughts together would be the only way we could all pass the class. We met every other night at the campus library to hash through the equations for upcoming exams. DiffyQs was such a mind- blowing class that we were given four equations to solve weeks prior to an exam, and we would still fail. One equation would take twelve to fifteen pages of meticulously written formulas, one after another, to solve. Even if you solved each formula correctly, one dropped negative, a derivative not carried out to the proper decimal point would destroy every step followed. It was maddening.

It was imperative that at least four of us came together. The study sessions went deep into the night for weeks. We shared the rotation of who was the lead, much like a flock of geese. Have you ever witnessed the "V" shape of geese migrating? A lead bird breaks the wind's path for the others to form behind. At intervals, the lead bird will drop from the front and take a spot in the back of the formation. This gives the lead bird a chance to rest as another moves forward to assume the lead. Give and take, ebb and flow, lead and follow. For us, sharing the leadership role created a growth atmosphere so that each of us could share our strengths while simultaneously following the lead of another.

Where in life have you used this construct and joined forces with a group of individuals to achieve a greater goal?

Another example of organized planning in my life is when my husband and I were living overseas in Geilenkirchen, Germany. We were a young military family living in a foreign country. Many of the airmen were about our same age and were also starting families. The husbands were constantly deploying to support the NATO mission in Bosnia. That left many of the spouses together to bond and explore the continent together. All the while, we were navigating it with our young children in tow. A group of mothers would come together twice a week to compare notes on child rearing, talk to the seasoned mothers, and basically learn from each other. We shared everything from baby digestive issues, potty training, language development, and more. This form of mastermind was established so that young mothers could gain a sense of readiness for whatever life would throw their way.

> *"Be stubborn about your goals and flexible with your methods."*
> *~ unknown*

Never underestimate the power of a tribe. This brings me to my final example of a mastermind. As an international keynote speaker, I have traveled to exotic places and met hundreds of amazing people with stories powerful enough to change the course of other lives. The stories I have collected belong to people I felt needed a platform to share their stories. They bear witness to transformation through trauma into success.

Furthermore, these stories show that the learning curve is not linear and that sometimes we take big steps backward to take greater strides forward. The book series, *Hold My Crown - Women of Grit Share Stories of Resilience* was born out of the necessity of women helping women. This mastermind has no boundaries and no walls to confine their thoughts. Through social media, we have reached around the world with the stories of resilience. Together, we share our journeys so that others will benefit from the lessons we share regardless of where they are in their life journey or where they reside. This mastermind will not stop at one book. There are plans to create a *Hold My Crown - Kings* edition with a continued compilation of Queens and Kings joining stories for future anthologies.

A Mastermind is more than a gathering of minds. It is a construct that allows the cultivation of thoughts, ideas, and plans to move into action and results. The coming together of diverse strengths and abilities helps foster fresh ideas. Organized planning is the oxygen that feeds the flames of desire into action.

"A dream written down with a date becomes goal.
A goal broken down into steps becomes a plan.
A plan backed by action makes your dreams come true."
~ Greg S. Reid

ABOUT MICHELLE MRAS

About Michelle Mras: Michelle is a Global Award-Winning Keynote & TEDx Speaker, Presentation Coach, co-Host of two podcasts: Denim & Pearls and Amplifluence. Michelle is the Host of MentalShift on The New Channel (TNC), Philippines. She's a multiple Best-Selling Author and co-Founder of Amplifuence - Amplifying the influence of Coaches, Authors and Speakers.

Michelle is a survivor of multiple life challenges to include a Traumatic Brain Injury and Breast Cancer. She guides others to recognize the innate gifts within them, stop apologizing for what they are not and step into who they truly are… Unapologetically.

Author's Website: *www.MichelleMras.com*
Book Series Website & Author's Bio: *www.The13StepstoRiches.com*

Mickey Stewart

YOUR FIELD OF DREAMS

IF YOU BUILD IT, he will come.

Often misquoted as "If you build it, they will come," this mantra from "Field of Dreams" has become a metaphor that has been the driving force behind many personal and business dreams.

Some of MY biggest dreams involved building something from nothing: building a new life in a foreign country, building a new home, and building online drumming courses—dreams which aren't for the faint-hearted, weak-minded, or easily distracted.

BUT what is the difference between those who follow through on their dreams and those who don't?

It's ORGANIZED PLANNING.

I know, ORGANIZED PLANNING doesn't sound super sexy, right? But just stay with me because I'm talking about BIG dreams. In such dreams, PayPal temporarily freezes withdrawals because there's SO much money pouring into your account that it's flagged as 'unusual activity.'

Yes, this actually happened to me! Let me explain.

Doing the immigration thing both ways (a few times) between Canada and the United Kingdom demanded a lot of patience, red tape, and tons of planning. Tearing down our old house to build four new homes (on the same plot of land) required a mind-spinning amount of planning. Building two hugely successful online bodhrán courses were all-consuming and took more planning, action, and faith than the other two combined. BUT the consistent, common thread that was weaved throughout all three initiatives was ORGANIZED PLANNING.

Napoleon Hill's ORGANIZED PLANNING chapter in *Think and Grow Rich* is filled with an incredible amount of information. Today, I'd like to laser in on two key pieces of advice that personally worked for me; it's where I believe most people get stuck when it comes to ORGANIZED PLANNING: ASK and ACTION!

Ask

1. Ask yourself the question, "What is it that I want?" and clearly declare your response in the form of a Definite Chief Aim.

If you've never written a Definite Chief Aim, it's important to know this step is CRITICAL to achieving organized planning success. Hill's detailed instructions for writing your Definite Chief Aim can be found in the Desire chapter of *Think and Grow Rich*. In short, he says:

"Write out a clear, concise statement of the amount of money you intend to acquire, name the time limit for its acquisition, state what you intend to give in return for the money, and describe clearly the plan through which you intend to accumulate it."

For example, the Definite Chief Aim I created for my first online bodhrán course read as follows:

"By my 39th birthday, May 19th, 2010, I have reached my goal of a £10,000 launch. I know I am giving my BEST material, and I am helping thousands of people learn bodhrán. I have listened to what my students wanted and sold my DVD as a hard copy and downloadable version. AND it was all easier than I ever could have imagined."

Creating this Definite Chief Aim resulted in me experiencing that PayPal scenario I mentioned above – causing them to temporarily freeze my withdrawals due to unusual activity (continuous amounts of money being poured into my account). Needless to say, this turned me into a Definite Chief Aim believer for life!

So, if there's one key thing that I could impart to you in this chapter, it's to be sure first to ASK yourself what you want (identifying your Definite Chief Aim) because you need to know WHERE YOU'RE GOING before you can make your plan. Your Definite Chief Aim is your destination, and ORGANIZED PLANNING is the vehicle that will take you on the road trip of a lifetime towards it. The clarity of your Definite Chief Aim - and the solidity of your plans to achieve it - will determine how well-calibrated your compass is for getting you there.

When you are clear on your Definite Chief Aim, you become magnetized to the ideas and plans you require to achieve it. I can't stress this enough. CLEAR, CONFIDENT, POWERFUL DECLARATIONS ARE MIND-BLOWINGLY EFFECTIVE! Not just for creating financial riches, but for creating a rich life. Immediately after writing my above Definite Chief Aim, EVERYTHING that I needed to build my first online bodhrán course - plans, people, systems, technology - started flooding in as if through a firehose.

Developing your Definite Chief Aim is an essential step in the planning process. Do not skip this! If you get busy 'doing' before your big road map is drawn, you'll drive around in circles – like Chevy Chase's character stuck in the roundabout in the movie *National Lampoon's European Vacation*.

Why is the mere act of writing your Definite Chief Aim so important? Because it's what propels you forward. Once you feel completely aligned with your goal and start seeing it as not just possible but inevitable, you'll immediately feel up-leveled, which causes you to WANT to take action.

2. Ask your ideal audience for input.

Here's what happened when I did this.

I had an email list of about 1,500 (at the time) and had only ever sent one message to them. They were grateful students who had been learning from me from my YouTube videos, and I had good engagement with them on that platform. So in my email, I asked them to tell me (exactly) what they wanted me to offer them in a course. Simple right? Ask people what they want and then provide it for them. It seems like a no-brainer, but it's a simple and obvious opportunity many people don't think to take advantage of.

To my surprise, I received an overwhelming number of responses to my short survey. Students disclosed the level of drummer they were; they shared the specific areas of drumming they struggled with, told me what they wanted more of, etc. In the end, SIX HUNDRED people I had never met took time out of their day to tell me exactly what they wanted! This survey feedback totally inspired me! It was as if lighter fluid had been added to a fire that was already lit under me. This kicked my ORGANIZED PLANNING into hyperdrive and helped me plan and put into motion the steps that would bring my first course to life.

Action

The pitfall I see many creatives fall into during the ORGANIZED PLANNING stage is analysis paralysis - getting stuck in the fear loop of 'over-thinking' to the point of being overwhelmed, which often results in NO action being taken. This is debilitating.

If you've been thinking about sharing your talent with the world but haven't managed to get around to it yet, please don't let 'overwhelm' cement you into analysis paralysis. And please be sure not to waste your life away not doing it because you fear what others might say. You're not going to be everyone's cup of tea, and that's ok. There are more than enough people in the world to go around, and you'll attract the people who resonate with your message.

So, what dream do YOU have that has yet to come true?

Now, imagine taking that vulnerable risk to put yourself out there to declare, "I'm going to create this thing," followed by dozens (or even hundreds) of people telling you that "if you build it, they will come"! I'd bet you'd have the same response I had, "Well, I better get going on this because now they're waiting for it!"

ACT! Start immediately. Ask yourself, "What is one small thing I can do to take action TODAY?" If even just that question throws you into analysis paralysis, and you know procrastination is your worst enemy, I suggest you get "The War of Art" by Steven Pressfield and read it. It's a powerful kick in the pants.

No matter how big (or small) your dreams may be, ORGANIZED PLANNING, beginning with asking yourself what you want and then taking action on it, is what makes the difference between those who follow through on their dreams and those who do not.

Tips For Building Your Field Of Dreams

1. Review Hill's detailed instructions for writing your Definite Chief Aim in the Desire chapter of *Think and Grow Rich*.
2. ASK yourself, "What is it that I want?" creating your Definite Chief Aim (posting it all over the place for you to see daily).
3. ASK your ideal audience for input.
4. Take ACTION. Get started building your plan right away.

If you build it, you're aligned with it, and people want it. And it's of value; they will come.

MICKEY STEWART

About Mickey Stewart: Born in Cape Breton, Canada, Mickey Stewart is a musician, coach, and author who has been a player and instructor of the snare drum and bodhrán for forty years.

Responsible for heading up the drum program at Ardvreck School in Perthshire, Scotland since 2002, Mickey is in high demand to teach throughout the U.K. and North America.

Creator and founder of BodhránExpert.com, her YouTube videos have received more than two million views from students and fans from every country throughout the world.

Over the past eight years, she's been involved in the TV and film industry as a supporting artist. Even more recently, she's begun following her newest passion, which is teaching others how to share their talents with the world.

Stewart lives in Crieff, Scotland with her husband of twenty-four years, Scottish musician and composer Mark Stewart, along with their 16-year-old son, Cameron, who is also a piper.

Author's Website: *www.MickeyStewart.com*
Book Series Website & Author's Bio: *www.The13StepstoRiches.com*

Natalie Susi

AN IDEA WITHOUT A PLAN IS JUST AN IDEA

When we have a vision for something that we want to bring to life, we need to organize inspired action steps to make that vision a reality. Organized planning is the leverage that enables your desired outcomes to manifest most efficiently and effectively. It is all about placement. Placing yourself in the right moment, around the right people and mentors, and in a position where you can consistently work towards your goal. The first step in this process is to get very clear on your desired outcome. Consider what it looks, sounds, and feels like to accomplish this goal. Write it down, visualize it, and really think about the details. Once this is done, create a game plan for how you will craft and cultivate your desire. It is important to get this plan checked and approved by like-minded people who will ignite your soul and push you to leverage yourself for the right opportunities. They should be people that will have your best interest in mind and be supportive yet realistic with you. Sometimes we feel as though we can carry all of the weight ourselves or know all the answers to our problems, but once we stop speaking and start listening, we can learn so much more.

Another quality you must embody is the persistence to keep going even when your ideal plan has failed or been disrupted. Life is all about pivoting. Change your plan, and rewrite your story, but whatever you do, do not fall into the trap of just giving up. I have persisted and rewritten my story multiple times throughout my entrepreneurial life. My first business was a total failure. I started an Italian Ice company in San Diego when no one knew what Italian Ice was or why I was trying to sell an ice cream product to people in the winter. That product was eventually rebranded into my next business, Bare Organic Mixers, an Organic cocktail mixer company. I ran that company for eight years, wore all of the business hats, learned all of my hard lessons through my failures and mistakes, and finally sold it to a natural foods company. It took almost a decade of my life, and while I'm grateful for the learning experience, it completely drained me, my relationships, and my bank account. I finally sold it when I woke up one day and realized that I no longer had a choice. I had to create a new vision to align with my purpose on the planet. It is always okay to change your ideas, business, and desires. It is not okay to lose your dreams, aspirations, and yourself. I sold my business to go back to teaching, the one thing that felt most natural and inspiring to me.

As I've mentioned in previous books, I didn't want to go back to traditional teaching and instruct on literature and writing. I wanted to teach and coach people on how to feel happier, uncover their triggers, patterns, and stuck points, and communicate from a place of love instead of fear. After selling my business, I got clear on my new vision around coaching and teaching, and then I put a game plan in place for how to start getting clients. I studied some of the best people in the coaching space and listened to their stories about how they started their businesses and created their coaching techniques. I assessed my strengths and weaknesses, what I was healthily obsessed with teaching, and what aspects of the business I never wanted to touch because I was simply not good at them.

When I first started coaching, I supported women going through breakups and wanted to start consciously dating. This content led me to help women develop their self-esteem, self-worth, and confidence. Then, I naturally evolved into what I'm doing now, coaching business owners on how to bridge communication gaps to be more in alignment with themselves, their vision, and their team members. The road to the ultimate vision shifted and changed a bit, but the end goal of helping people with my natural ability and desire to teach stayed the same. I still have goals for new businesses I am developing, and I have accepted that it is okay to adjust your plan. It is okay to take a few steps back, go back to the drawing board, read more books, and learn from mentors.

Persistence is key here, but it is not enough. When having the desired outcome, you also need to identify if your plans are practical and workable since this leads to being persistent. As I mentioned above, I had to constantly change my plans and redefine what my purpose in business was. Many of us think we can become successful if we run a business. But the truth is if it is not realistic and if you are not flexible with improving and readjusting your plan, it will not work out the way you want it to. You will become stuck and exhausted, and it will feel like you are constantly pushing a boulder up a hill instead of being in flow with your skills and on a mission with your purpose.

This leads to my next point of temporary defeat. Defeat is a beautiful thing if you use it to your advantage and reframe your failure. Defeat does not mean that there is a problem with you. It does not mean that you are not capable enough, that you are not worthy enough, or that you will never get enough. On the contrary, defeat is an opportunity for growth. Period. Endnote. The temporary disappointment will pass. Your plans just need some tweaking and refinement.

Our thoughts become our reality. If you have faith in your manifestation and desires, they will begin to cultivate. Affirmations have become a big part of my daily practice. They help reassure me that I will receive what I desire, that the universe is on my side, that everything will be okay, and that I am exactly where I am supposed to be. This has helped me stay grounded and aligned during challenging times.

Self-awareness is just as important. Completing an analysis of my strengths and weaknesses has helped me get in tune with my purpose with coaching and has enabled me to see how I can help others most efficiently and effectively. I knew the beverage industry was not meant for me, and I transitioned into holistic coaching that allowed my strengths to flourish. Be honest with yourself about the areas you lack and the areas that you can improve quickly. Get clear on where you shine. What tasks or activities feel like a natural fit for you? What do you genuinely enjoy doing, and what do you always dread? What feels easy and in flow, and what feels really daunting and hard?

Finally, always remember that giving as much as you receive is important. When you continue to give humbly and create genuine relationships with others, you will receive an abundance of blessings. Have faith that you will achieve your desired outcome. I hope my story can inspire you that you can do it too.

Below is a short exercise to help you start brainstorming and completing this organized planning process:

What is your desired outcome? What does it look and sound and feel like? Why do you want this desired outcome? Why does it matter to you?

What are some of your first action steps?

Who are some of the best people you can speak to about this desired outcome? Why are these people a great fit to speak with?

Can you anticipate any stuck points or obstacles you might run into? What are they, and what will you do to work around them?

What are your strengths and weaknesses as it pertains to this desired outcome? What do you love to do? What do you dread doing? What is your zone of genius?

How does this desired outcome align with your purpose on the planet? Why does it inspire you?

NATALIE SUSI

About Natalie Susi: Natalie has more than 14 years of experience as a teacher, speaker, entrepreneur and mentor. Currently she's a 5-year UCSD professor focusing on communications and the Pursuit of Happiness. As an entrepreneur, she founded and grew Bare Organic Mixers beverage company for 8 years resulting in an acquisition in 2014.

After selling the company, Natalie combined her educational background as a teacher and her experience as an entrepreneur to provide personal development coaching and consulting to individuals, businesses, and creative entrepreneurs. She developed a program called Conscious Conversations and utilizes a step-by-step process called The Alignment Method to support leaders in cultivating conscious teams and businesses through a process of self-reflection, self-discovery, and self-ascension that ultimately increases profits, productivity, and the growth of the individuals personally and professionally.

Author's website: *www.NatalieSusi.com*
Book Series Website & Author's Bio: *www.The13StepsToRiches.com*

Nita Patel

YOUR PLAN REQUIRES ACTION

According to Napoleon Hill, organized planning is the sixth step towards riches. It's the crystallization of desire into action through strategic steps.

Step 1 –   Know the qualities of a great leader
Step 2 –   Select the right leaders to surround yourself with
Step 3 –   Mastermind with them regularly
Step 4 –   Plan, Plan, Plan
Step 5 –   Know that temporary defeat is a part of the process
Step 6 –   Stay committed and take action daily towards your plan

Step 1

There is NO such thing as a self-made millionaire. No one can become rich on their own. It takes clients, customers, partners, teams, supporters, cheerleaders, etc. If we were truly self-made, the world wouldn't exist as it does today. But more on that in a philosophy book.

Who do you look up to? Whom do you want to be like? What are the qualities you're looking to adopt? And which qualities are going to contribute to your success? As you may have read in previous volumes of this series, my journey started with watching The Secret, which led me to read books like *Think and Grow Rich* by Napoleon Hill. When you can't find people to associate with in person, reading their books, doing their online programs, and joining virtual communities is the next best option. That is what I did. I bought personal development programs from John Assaraf, Sonia Ricotti, Bob Proctor, Vishen Lakiani's MindValley platform, and many other sources, to name a few. I spent a few years here. I joined a Mastermind facilitated by Bob Proctor, where I met other incredible like-minded individuals who uplifted me. There was one quality or strength in all these individuals which I desired to adopt. Not everything is for everyone. And not every quality of these individuals was something I desired.

Bob Proctor taught me the concept of abundance. Sonia Ricotti introduced me to the concept of forgiveness and how to practice it. John Assaraf taught me that it's possible to reprogram your subconscious mind. These were all strengths I imbibed through their teachings.

Step 2

Your network is your net worth.

Take inventory. We are the average of the five people we spend the most time with. As I progressed through my personal development journey, I noticed that many people fell out of my circle. Not on purpose, but it was a natural progression of events that led to an organic shift in my network. My inner circle changed. The random occurrences of whom I met at an event changed. I experienced a profound shift from uneasy, walking on eggshell relationships to influential leaders with open arms and a warm heart willing to support me in any capacity.

One day I was approached by a wonderful and enthusiastic gentleman named Erik Swanson. He invited me to join his mastermind, and through this mastermind, I was invited to join an excellent book series called The *13 Steps to Riches.* Being a part of this book series opened doors to a whole new world. I was now co-authoring with the people I had been following online and whose books I was reading!

Even if you're not in the place you want to be today, create a virtual or mental relationship with the leaders you admire and wish to associate with. The laws of the universe will undeniably give you what you ask for and so much more beyond belief.

Step 3

Napoleon Hill used to have imaginary meetings with people like Carnegie, Ford, Edison, Lincoln, and others long before he started working for Carnegie and eventually met many men he mentally associated with.

I thought one day that I, too, wanted to meet some of the members of the documentary *The Secret*. After several conversations justifying why this was an acceptable thought, I decided that I was ready to meet them. Within a few weeks, I had a run-in with Mr. Swanson. I chose to speak up in a conversation with him, and I was immediately invited to his brilliant mastermind, where I met these incredible leaders.

Step 4

As with anything, execution becomes simpler when you take the time to plan. Do you want to become an author? How will you write a book? I used to coach authors to write their books in 90 days, and the biggest challenge was teaching authors how to integrate it into their daily life, so it was not an overwhelming process. It required discipline and planning. Either take 20 minutes to write every morning before your day starts so your mind is clear of any chaos from the day, or take 3-4 hours on a Saturday or Sunday morning and go to a park, trail, or someplace in nature where focus and creativity come naturally. Without this plan, you will tend to procrastinate because the task seems so overwhelming. This bite-size plan allows you to integrate new projects into your daily schedule. When one project is completed, it will feel good to start the next without feeling overwhelmed.

Step 5

Temporary defeat is always a part of the plan. If success came the first time you tried something, the Mediterranean Sea would be crowded with yachts. Success comes with plans and implementing systems to execute, but it also takes perseverance. The first conversation may not win you a sale in business, and a B2B sale can take up to 100+ days. But, each time, you learn from the conversation and come back more prepared with resolutions to the clients' needs. It doesn't happen in one shot, and it takes patience and perseverance.

Step 6

Remember the Seinfeld episode where Kramer was so upset that someone else stole his idea? When I re-watched that episode many years later, I thought of how I felt when I saw modern or contemporary art. There's a famous art phrase, "modern art - I could do that. Yeah, but you didn't". That episode made me think of that quote. That was when I realized I needed to start investing my time in exploring my creativity because whether I did it or not, others would continue theirs, and I would continue thinking, "I could do that."

Take action daily. As I mentioned in step 4, when you break down a big project like writing a book into 20 minutes a day at a set time every day, it becomes a part of your routine and will get done. No matter how many shower ideas you have consistently if you're not acting on any of them, someone else will.

With these six steps, your dream has no chance but to manifest into your reality.

NITA PATEL

About Nita Patel: Nita is a best-selling author, speaker, and artist who believes in modern etiquette as a path to becoming our best selves.

Through her professional years, Ms. Patel has 25 years of demonstrated technology leadership experience in various industries specifically with a concentrated focus in health care for 14 of those 20+ years. She's shown her art across the world to include the Louvre in Paris. She's a best-selling author and performance coach, pursuing her master's in Industrial organizational (I-O) psychology at Harvard. Her investment in psychology theory and practice is what led her to a deep interest in helping others. She has become deeply and passionately devoted to nurturing others and in building their confidence and brand through speaking and consultative practices.

Author's Website: *www.Nita-Patel.com*
Book Series Website & Author's Bio: *www.The13StepstoRiches.com*

Olga Geidane

DITCH BEING ORGANIZED

Why You Should Never Prepare for the Wedding Day

People spend months and sometimes even years preparing for the perfect wedding day, and it usually ends up being just right! So amazing to the point where everything is matching, and every single detail is thought of (are you yawning yet?).

I wish those couples would spend at least a quarter of that invested time preparing for the marriage. Then the divorce rate would finally drop!

The minute the wedding is over - those newlyweds are left to themselves, hoping for the happy ever after and facing the reality of filing for a divorce before even the 10th wedding anniversary (or even first, let's be honest!).

Why would I bring this wedding example here, in the personal development book on Organized Planning?

Well, firstly, because it is just a PERFECT example of how failing to plan for marriage (rather just one wedding day) ends up in preparing for failing.

And the second reason why I brought it up here is that it's the story of my first marriage too - and it didn't last for long! Is that you too?

So let's go back to the main purpose of this chapter: to help you achieve more in life even if you are not an organized person!

In fact, I should have mentioned that earlier: this is for those who want to ditch being organized and have more fun in life while achieving what they want in life!

Remember, there are many reasons WHY you are not organized, and one of them is that your mind is very creative, which is AMAZING, so that is exactly what you can use to become more successful!

So let's start with the basics:

- What's the craziest thing you would like to happen (so-called "end goal")?
- What are your best skills in this to come true? (basically, what are your strengths)?
- Who can complement your skill set, so you don't do what you have zero desire to do (that's your team)?
- Who knows who and what, and where (creating your inner circle of trusted people)?
- Play full out (in other words, give 100% in everything you do)!
- Think of the impact of your choices BEFORE you make them!
- Stay curious or become a tree!

Here I will explain every one of the points in detail.

FIRST: What's the craziest thing you would like to happen (so-called "end goal")? Forget the boring "where do you see yourself in 10 years". Think fun, big and exciting, in a way, "if THIS happened, it would BLOW MY MIND!".

Why?

Why not? I know for years they educate us on being very pragmatic and pre-plan everything but guess what? We live in a new world, and some of the stuff, frankly, just got too old and boring. I don't want to think about my exact net worth at XYZ age. Instead, I want to think, "Geez. If I manage to visit every single country on Earth while transforming people's lives and enjoying financial freedom, I would be the happiest person!"

Some might say that it is the same as having a money goal. No, it's not.

Not everyone is motivated by money. You might be. I am not. And it took me two decades to understand that. If your craziest thing is to be the first billionaire in a family, so be it, but don't join the herd of people saying, "you must think of a money goal," if that is not what motivates you.

And now, breathe! As I know that for many, that is very liberating! At least it was for me at the time!

SECOND: What are your best skills in this to come true? (basically, what are your strengths)? Why is that important? Let me ask you this question: would you like to do MORE and BORING work or LESS and FUN?

I know the answer; it never changes across the nations and races: LESS AND FUN, OLGA! Well, in that case, take a pen and some paper and write down what you are so good at that people constantly ask you for help with. What are you praised for? What is the thing that YOU KNOW you are awesome and effortless at? What's your talent? What's your gift?

So in my case, while I want to visit every country on Earth while transforming people's lives and enjoying financial freedom. I must remember my strengths: my coaching skills, intuition, expertise, life experience, great listening skills, humor, compassion, public speaking and presentation talent, motivational nature, positivity, high energy, photography, etc. There is no right or wrong when it comes to your skills. It is about knowing what YOU are really-really-really good at. Often you would also enjoy your skills as they are your second nature.

What about the rest of the things and skills, you might wonder? And this is where the third part comes in!

THIRD: Who can complement your skill set so you don't do what you have zero desire to do? (let's build your team). The rest of the people who have passion and talents for what you don't have - can do what they are best at!

You might think that is cruel; making other people do what you don't like doing!

But something YOU LOVE being busy with is other people's worst nightmare!

For example, I am very analytical, and I LOVE getting to the bottom of everything, someone's problem, new information, historical event, personality trait, disease, etc. So give me anything, and I will dive right into it! I can imagine the faces of some people reading this; they will be like, "Nah, I will scratch the surface and leave the rest to others!"

Remember, there is a person in the world for everything you can't or don't know how to do - that other people are LOVING to deal with! Let them plan, schedule, etc.

So keep them busy and happy while you are moving closer to your craziest thing!

FORTH: Who knows who and what and where? (creating your inner circle of trusted people). There was a time when information was the most valuable thing, as there was a deficit in the sources. Society still believes in that. The truth is, YOUR INNER CIRCLE is what is more worthy now than the information you can acquire. Make sure that in addition to the people in your team helping you passionately with things you don't shine at, you have trusted people who know MORE than you! You want them to have more experience than you, at least!

Someone said: if you are the smartest person in the room, you are in the wrong room!

Whenever I hear from the event organizer that I was the best speaker by far, I know I must raise the quality of speakers with whom I share my stage (virtual and in-person!).

FIFTH: Play full out (in other words, give 100% in everything you do)! "If we do it, we do it!" Often, we say it with my husband because we believe in living and giving beyond 100%! When we work, we do it full-on. We overdeliver. When we take care of each other, we go 100%, and beyond that, when we party and travel and have fun, again, we do it beyond 100%!

Why?

Why not?

Every time you give far and beyond 100%, one way or another, the Universe will pour all the abundance and alignment right back at you!

You will be noticed and recognized; you will be thanked and reciprocated, remembered, etc. Do you need any more reasons?

However, there is something you MUST remember when you go full-on…

SIXTH: Think of the impact of your choices BEFORE you make them! A great movie to watch and learn from on how NOT to make choices is *The Wolf of Wall Street* (with Leonardo Di Caprio)! I know many watched that movie and didn't analyze it, but I did (remember, Olga is VERY analytical and wants to know where is the beginning of all)! So do me a favor, watch that movie again, observe, learn, see and hear how people in the movie are making their choices and what they led to.

"Hindsight is a wonderful thing, but foresight is better, especially when it comes to saving a life," said William Blake. And you, dear reader, are saving your life and many other people's lives every day (often in a long-term way) when you make a decision!

SEVENTH: Be curious or become a tree! What happens to a tree that stops growing, expanding its roots and branches?

It starts dying. Period.

Stay curious in life, wonder, experiment, and be open-minded.

You might wonder why this is the shortest point of all - that's just to keep you curious!

I FORGOT to mention that those seven points were the formula for the most disorganized person on how to still succeed in life. But knowing that most likely you would just skip that line, I decided to skip that, too. At the end of the day, I am not the most organized person, either!

So here is my question to your busy and creative mind: How long more will you live the life you have lived so far?

Go ahead, apply those seven steps and email me to Olga@newlifekickstart. com your stories. It's always fun reading those, and I promise to respond personally. And I will tell you what happened on the day of my second marriage; you won't believe it!

OLGA GEIDANE

About Olga Geidane: Olga is an International Speaker, an Event MC/Host, Facilitator, Mindset Coach, a Best-Selling Author, and a Regional President of the Professional Speaking Association in the UK. She is a host of Olga's Show and A World-Traveler.

Olga helps ambitious people to unlock their extraordinary performance and their true, authentic side. She is passionate about helping people to live their best lives. Olga knows how tough it is to be broke and unfulfilled in life: at the age of 24, just after her divorce, Olga came to the UK from Latvia with no spoken English, with just £100 in her pocket and a 2.5-year-old son. Olga is a very inspirational survivor: she went through abuse, betrayal, cheating, financial loss and emotional breakdown. Matt Black (Business Model Innovation & Disruption Consultant - Snr. Advisor to CEO, CSO, CCO, COO - Author & International Public Speaker) said: "Olga really takes it up a notch beyond anything I have seen before. She is one of the bravest people I have ever seen on stage. If you are looking to book a speaker or attend a talk that will be inspiring, challenging and leave you wanting to take action... She is perfect."

Author's Website: *www.OlgaGeidane.com*
Book Series Website & Author's Bio: *www.The13StepstoRiches.com*

Paul Andrés

THE SECRET SAUCE TO SUCCESS

What is organized planning and how can it help you to be successful?

Well, for me, organized planning has been the secret sauce to all of my personal success. It has been the key element in the process for me to truly pull together my genius systematically to plan, review, analyze and make any adjustments as necessary to ensure the final outcome is, in fact, successful. Organized planning is no new concept by any means. It has been around for centuries and has been used by some of the most successful people in history. One of the earliest examples of organized planning comes from none other than Napoleon Hill himself. In his book, *"The Law of Success,"* Hill outlines what he calls the "Master Plan." This Master Plan is essentially a blueprint for success that can be applied to any area of life.

The Master Plan consists of four main steps:

1. Define your purpose
2. Set your goals
3. Make a plan
4. Take action

While these four steps may seem simple enough, the execution of these steps is key. And this is where organized planning comes in. You see, without a plan, it is very easy to get sidetracked or discouraged. But with a plan, you have a roadmap to follow that will keep you on track and help you to stay focused on your goals.

So what does organized planning look like in action? Let's take a closer look at each of the four steps outlined in the Master Plan.

1. **Define your purpose:** This step is all about getting clear on what you want to achieve. What is your end goal? What are your ambitions and dreams? Once you have a good understanding of your purpose, you can begin to set goals that will help you to achieve it.

2. **Set your goals:** This step is all about setting specific, measurable, achievable, relevant, and time-bound goals. These are the goals that you will work towards in your plan. It is important to make sure that your goals are realistic and achievable. Otherwise, you will likely become discouraged.

3. **Make a plan:** This step is all about putting your goals into action. What specific steps do you need to take to achieve your goals? You will need to create a timeline for each goal and identify what tasks need to be completed and by when. This is where having a planner or a system to keep track of your progress can be very helpful.

4. **Take action:** This is the most important step of all. You will need to take consistent and determined action to achieve your goals. This means taking small but steady steps towards your goal on a daily basis. Remember, Rome wasn't built in a day, and neither are successful businesses or careers. It takes time, patience and consistency to achieve great things.

And never forget that no plan is ever set in stone, and there will always be unforeseen circumstances that come up along the way. The ability to adapt and change as needed separates the successful from the unsuccessful. It's this flexibility that makes it possible for mistakes to remain just that, mistakes, instead of catastrophic even and huge downfalls. Life happens, and things change, and with organized planning, you can easily make adjustments along the way to ensure your success.

By definition, it is the process of creating a plan to achieve a specific goal. This process can be used in any area of life, whether personal or professional. The important thing to remember is that organized planning is not a one-time event, but rather it is a continuous process that should be revisited on a regular basis.

The benefits of organized planning are numerous, but some of the most notable include:
  – improved time management
  – increased productivity
  – better goal setting and achievement
  – improved decision making
  – reduced stress levels

Ok, so now that we know what organized planning is and why it's important, let's look at how we can use it to achieve success.

There are several different ways that people can use organized planning to achieve success. First, it's important to make sure that you have defined your goals clearly and precisely. This means that you should list everything you want to achieve and then break those goals down into smaller, more manageable pieces. Once you have done this, you can start developing a plan of action to achieve each goal.

It's also important to make sure that you have all of the resources you need to achieve your goals. This means that you should take inventory of your skills, knowledge, experience, and the resources you have available to you. Once you have done this, you can start developing a plan for acquiring or developing the resources you need to achieve success.

Organized planning is also about setting deadlines and holding yourself accountable. You should set a date for when you want to achieve each goal and then make sure that you stick to that deadline. It's also important to keep track of your progress along the way and make sure that you are making the necessary adjustments to your plan as you go. This will help you ensure that you are on track to achieve your goals and help you identify any potential problems along the way.

It can be helpful to think of organized planning as a road map. Just as a road map helps you see the best route from Point A to Point B, organized planning can help you see the best way to achieve your goals. By identifying the steps you need to take and the resources you'll need along the way, organized planning makes it possible to develop a clear and actionable plan that will help you achieve your desired results.

By breaking down your goals into manageable steps and working towards them one at a time while also ensuring that all of the resources necessary for success are available when needed, you will see success time and time again. This allows you to focus on what's important--achieving your goals--while at the same time knowing that everything else is working to support your efforts. Whether you are a student looking to get into your dream school, an entrepreneur trying to start your own business, or just in need of some guidance as you navigate through life's ups and downs, organized planning is a powerful tool that can help to guide you along the way to your ultimate success.

Ultimately, organized planning is a key component of success because it allows you to create an action plan to help you reach your goals over time. If you want to be successful, organized planning is the secret sauce you need. It will help you stay on track and focused, even when the going gets tough, to make significant progress towards achieving your dreams. Just be sure to put your plan in place, work consistently toward it over time, and don't give up when things get difficult! With organized planning as your guide, there's no limit to what you can achieve. So why not give it a try? You just might be surprised by the results!

PAUL ANDRÉS

About Paul Andrés: Paul is an award-winning conscious entrepreneur, visual storyteller, and intuitive coach. From digital and interior design, to business clarity and personal growth coaching, to social justice advocacy and volunteering, Andrés is proof that aligning your passions with your purpose is the true magic to success. He currently devotes his time to helping awakened entrepreneurs and heart-centered creatives design the life they deserve through personal and professional coaching and consulting, as well as shedding light on uncomfortable topics that bring awareness to the social justice issues of today as the host of his video podcast, *In Your Mind*. Andrés is also a two-time #1 best-selling author. You can catch him as a featured guest speaker at events across the country.

"Home is so many things, but ultimately, it's where life happens. It's where we sleep and grow a family, it's where we play and grow professionally, and it's where we learn and grow within. Each home plays a key role in helping us design a whole life—the life we all deserve." — *Paul Andrés*

Author's Website: *www.PaulAndres.com*
Purchase Book Online: *www.The13StepstoRiches.com*

Paul Capozio

PLAN YOUR NEXT STEP

In *Think and Grow Rich,* Napoleon Hill describes that we need to see that those plans we make are checked and approved by the members of your mastermind alliance. No follower of this philosophy can reasonably expect to accumulate a fortune without experiencing temporary defeat.

The Sixth step to riches is a sound, sure step. It is the foundation upon which everything else is built. Napoleon Hill tells us repeatedly in his materials: "Organized planning is the crystallization of desire into action; the molding of aspiration into reality; the creation of a big, broad airplane that will carry you over all obstacles on your journey toward the goal of riches."

A Total Mastermind Alliance is required to make organized planning possibly effective and full of prosperity. Methodical planning crystallizes desire into action. Whether you write it down, visualize it, or confide in others, your specific plans are the roadmap to success on all accounts.

The successful person has a definite objective in mind concerning what he is trying to accomplish. He selects the right kind of plan and makes his plans so undeniable that they may be reduced to writing. He then begins to put his plan into action. He refuses to permit himself to become discouraged or disheartened by possible defeats and failures. He knows that all such setbacks are temporary and must necessarily be encountered on the way to success. He also knows that these temporary defeats and losses are not nearly as dangerous or insurmountable as the attitude of mind that permits these defeats and failures to discourage you and make you feel defeated before you start.

Hill describes that we need to see that those plans we make are checked and approved by the members of your mastermind alliance. "No Follower of this philosophy can reasonably expect to accumulate a fortune without experiencing temporary defeat," Mr. Hill said.

"Riches" are man's universal desire. All desire it and strive for it, but few understand the road to riches.

You've now learned that each step has such a unique yet decisive role in acquiring riches.

Step 1:   Desire - Keep alive in your consciousness the DESIRE for money until it has become a dominating obsession.

Step 2:   Faith - Visualization and Belief in the Attainment of Desire.

Step 3:   Auto Suggestion - The Medium for Influencing the Subconscious.

Step 4:   Specialized Knowledge - Personal Experiences or Observations.

Step 5:   Imagination - The Workshop of the Mind.

Step 6:   Organized Planning - The Crystallization of Desire into Action.

As you plan your next steps in the process and journey of acquiring riches, carefully consider your plan and the actions you will take as the foundational stepping stones of wealth and prosperity. With these foundational pieces, the principles that riches are built on are all part of one big plan to help others throughout the journey and after you will achieve it.

PAUL CAPOZIO

About Paul Capozio: Paul Capozio was born in Hoboken, New Jersey and grew up on the streets of Hudson County. At 35, he was recruited to be the President of Sales and Marketing for a 350-million-dollar human resources firm. In seven years, he drove the top line revenue of that firm to over 1.5 billion.

Capozio owns and operates Capco Capital, Inc., an investment and consulting firm. The majority of Capco's holdings are of manufacturers and distributors of health and wellness products and human resources firms. Capco provides sales consulting and training, helping companies increase sales through traditional and direct sales disciplines. Making the invisible visible and simplifying the complex is his stock and trade.

A dynamic public speaker, he provides motivation and "meat and potatoes" skills to those in the health and wellness field who do not consider themselves "salespeople," allowing their voices to be heard above the "noise."

He is a husband of 32 years to his wife, Linda. He is also a father and grandfather.

Author's Website: *www.PaulCapozio.com*
Purchase Book Online: www. *The13StepstoRiches.com*

Phillip McClure

THE MIND MAPS

"The trouble with not having a goal is that you can spend your life
running up and down the field and never score."
~ Bill Copeland

Goals are very important. Equally important is having the ability to be flexible while moving towards your goals. This is much more difficult than one may believe, and almost everyone who has found success in their plan has had to adapt it along the way. You come up with an idea, you love it, your friends love it, but for some reason, it is not catching fire, and the company or idea is not achieving the success you know it should be getting. Then you meet someone, and they tell you that you should rip your entire business plan apart and start over because "the way you are running your business is incorrect." "You are in the subscription and membership business; you are not a store." Of course, you hear this after spending significant time and money building the website, advertising social media, and buying the products. Then, someone tells you to start over.

The requirement to be flexible and learn to adapt and correct your course comes into effect. Take that criticism and continue to move forward toward your goal. This was the story of my company. It took me a year of hard work to get it where I wanted it to be. I thought I knew so much, and all at once, I was excited and deflated because someone highlighted for me many of the things I did not know. This is the value and the power of an accountability partner, a mastermind, and the use of your mind maps.

Mind mapping out your goals will clarify what you're working on and continue your motivation as you keep moving closer to your goals. It breaks down the question: When I'm making a decision, is the decision aligned with my goals?

Once your mind map is complete, it is a useful technique to show it to an accountability buddy or your mastermind group. Not only will this give you feedback on what you're trying to accomplish, but often it assists you in accelerating achieving your goals. For example, I was having difficulty finding a company to build a membership platform for my online business. Every company I attempted to work with could not add the last little feature I was trying to capture. One of my accountability partners looked at the mind map I had written out to reach 5,000 members and said, "Hey, that's what my friend's company specializes in." They gave me their number, and the issue was easily taken care of. I wasted many hours going back and forth with companies online, only to find out they actually could not perform the required task. I wish I had shown this earlier and relied on the expertise of others.

You need to be in the ideal environment to reach your goals. When you find yourself around only people who are asking you for help, who have goals that do not match up to any of the goals or level of the goals you are striving for, you are in the wrong circle. Look at the people who are achieving the goals you are pursuing. Where do they eat, live, socialize, and what are their hobbies? If you want to learn from them and be like them, you must do the things they do.

You have likely already recognized that people with and without money often like the same things. Every day you meet people with whom you share interests and could probably hang out with and have a good time. Based on this alone, you might never know whether this person is a multimillionaire or that they are down to their last ten bucks until their next paycheck rolls around. You are most likely incorrect if you think you are not good enough or do not know how to talk to people you may be trying to emulate. You are in your own head, beating yourself up and allowing negativity to build. Instead, recognize your own greatness, tell yourself that you are good enough, that you are like them, but that you just have some more to learn. Once you change your mindset, the next part is to find a way into their circles and put yourself in that environment. Then the big key is to BE YOURSELF. Talk about the things you like, and you will find that new circle of people with the same interests. If you like Star Trek, talk about that and see if it connects, or boxing, fishing, Hawaii, whatever it might be. Connect with them in conversation and you may teach them something in return.

Education and time are major differences between who you are and whom you want to become. This is not referring to only conventional education but also learning something in an area you are interested in and becoming a subject matter expert in it. Creating positive habits and better discipline will assist you with gaining a higher knowledge of financial and business intelligence. This takes time but can be accelerated the more time you spend in the environment where you will naturally fit in the future. Spending time socializing in the circles you want your future self to be in will allow you to become that person sooner. The more time you put yourself out there to make the right friends and connections, the faster you will assimilate into that lifestyle. Remember, you often only need to make one good connection. This connection will make the rest for you.

You will see a fillable example on a basic mind map taken out of the *NorthStar Coins Journal* on the following page. It can be used for almost any type of goal attainment, whether in weight loss, wealth building, or business growth. These are all things that we work with every day, and we need to have a plan to follow to achieve the goals.

northstarcoins.com

MIND MAP INSTRUCTIONS

Mind maps have many applications, such as helping to calm anxiety, improving focus, solving problems, and creating goals.

In the largest bubble, write a main point that you want to focus on. Take some time to think about it.

In the medium bubbles, write the things that contribute to your main point. Try to break down your main point into smaller more manageable pieces.

In the smallest bubbles, write the things that contribute to your medium bubbles. Break down each medium thought into the smallest, most manageable form.

After completing your mind map take some time to ground yourself. Use your physical senses. What sounds can you hear around you? What can you smell? What can you taste? Be aware of how your body feels. Try to release some of the tension you body may be holding. Take three deep breaths; in through your nose and out through your mouth.

northstarcoins.com

PHILLIP D. MCCLURE

About Phillip D. McClure: Phillip is married to the love of his life, Maaike McClure, and is a very proud father of two exciting kids. He was raised in the Great state of Montana before moving to Utah. Phil lives life to the fullest. His accomplishments consist completing a full Ironman, deploying four times with the Army, earning multiple decorations along the way. Including two Utah crosses! Which makes him the only soldier in history to receive that medal twice. Currently, Phil is the Owner of NorthStar Coins, Events by NorthStar, the co-owner of P.B. Fast cars and recruits pilots for the Army Aviation program. It was during his last deployment that he accidentally created his first mastermind and it has forever changed his life as well as the others involved. He mentors and coaches in self-improvement and physical fitness.

Phil is an exotic-car enthusiast who spends as much time behind the wheel as possible, whether it is carving through canyons, ripping around the racetrack, or coaching others to see their potential. Competitive driving is the best therapy in the world.

Live life to the fullest and have fun while doing it. You don't get a rewind in life so take mistakes as the lessons they are and improve, don't make the same mistakes twice.

Live in flow, not with the flow.

Authors website: *www.NorthStarCoins.com*
Book Series Website & Author's Bio: *www.The13StepsToRiches.com*

Robyn Scott

GRAB YOUR P.A.I.L.

Organized planning is one of the most talked-about subjects in my first Best Selling book: *"Bringing People Together: Rediscovering the Lost Art of Face to Face Connecting, Collaborating and Creating."* I feel that this is applicable in most situations with business, not just for planning "spectaculous" events!

The Four Pillars of Powerful Planning include impactful information like:

1. **Commitment**
   - Commitments vs. expectations
   - Setting goals, results, intentions
   - The power of choice and courage
   - Your unique contribution

2. **Clarity**
   - Bringing people together on your terms
   - Human patterns
   - Knowing your tribe or avatar
   - Solving people's pain points and desires
   - Audience building
   - Attracting and repelling on purpose

3. **Creation**
   - Creating an experience vs. (an event)
   - Essence of the location and event

- The importance of proximity
- Leaving a lasting impact
- Interaction and participation

4. Communion
- Seeing it all come together
- What to do when you get there
- Making a difference with people
- Creating lasting impressions and relationships
- Causing constant growth

When you are planning (an event), I want you to consider, write down, start with, and base the rest of your planning on your highest-level commitments. The commitments that you have that never go away. You subconsciously act in line with these commitments constantly.

When we are brave enough to start bringing people together, it takes courage to make the invitations and plans. We literally and figuratively "put ourselves out there," which takes something from us to organize (an event). In a sense, we are taking a risk. The commitment to stay comfortable and safe constantly operates in the background. We are primal creatures, and so survival is always a present instinct.

When we practice any type of courage, our survival mechanisms get triggered. Fight or flight comes into consideration. This commitment subconsciously sabotages our bravery or responsibility. We often say we want to do something, and if it gets scary or uncomfortable, we are tempted to back out, create problems, distract ourselves, or find reasons and excuses not to follow through on our plans.

Have you ever noticed that happening? In retrospect, can you catch yourself where you've done that in life before? You must come to know, understand, and accept this human behavior so that you don't let it stop you in your commitment to making a difference with your mission to host an amazing gathering.

As you begin to bring people together, I would love to teach you a valuable tool I call PAIL. It is your equation for a conscious gathering. You are a conscious creative Connection Catalyst! You must take responsibility for this role. You must own this identity as you create an impactful event. Whenever you want to get back to consciousness and authentic creation, grab your PAIL and get to planning.

Letter "P" is for Purpose. Much like your commitment, you must know the purpose of your event. Map it out. Write it out. List out all the factors that are driving your purpose for this event! Know the purpose of the event and how the purpose of this specific event is aligned with your overall life commitments. This may be a commitment for you personally. It may also be commitments for your brand, your mission, your movement, or simply your life. Whatever it is, always be sure to start with purpose and commitment.

Letter "A" is for Alignment. Be sure that your purpose and event are aligned with your own standards. The desires of your audience are vital to a successful event. You can pack the room, and if your event is out of alignment with the attendees, it will be lackluster. People may leave early or post bad reviews online.

Each factor of events from start to finish is important. At no point do I encourage a coordinator to think that just because the doors have opened means you made it. Follow through all the way to the last follow-up. This is important in making sure you are in alignment. Follow-up and follow-through will ensure a great event that people will talk about for years.

Letter "I" is for impact. Know your impact before your guests do. How your event is going to impact people shouldn't be a mystery. What experience do you want to create? What memories do you want to create? How do you want to impact each heart that attends your event? As we get deeper and deeper into this book, I will get more specific about whom you are serving and how you are serving them. Knowing the impact early makes the whole process more impactful!

Please do not take impact lightly. If you've ever attended one powerful gathering, you know that an event can completely change someone's entire life's direction, focus, and trajectory. Please do not treat this fact casually. The concept of bringing people together is to save lives. It is to remind people that they are not alone. It is to encourage the connection of humanity. You will have a mighty impact on lives. So know it, own it, love it, and live it with pride and honor.

Letter "L" is for Legacy. Much like impact, the legacy you leave will outlast your body. It will last long after your event ends. The words that you say or how you look into somebody's eyes after their big "aha" moment will mark a forever stamp on their life. This concept is so magical when you think about it. Your bravery and courage to bring people together contribute to humanity. Your saving or transforming one person's life makes a difference for decades.

Leaving a legacy is about living with integrity. Keeping your promises to yourself to live out your dreams is leading by example and poise. Put your heart into each occasion, knowing that you will make a difference and create a ripple effect that has no boundaries.

If you plan your event with **PAIL,** I can guarantee that it will make a greater difference than you could ever imagine.

To wrap up this chapter of the Commitment Pillar, if you have not already, I would like to encourage you to write yourself a mission statement! Whether a mom, an entrepreneur, a doctor, a teacher, or whatever, writing a personal and professional mission statement will empower your entire life! And if you get it right, your mission statement and life will be one and the same! This approach is from a space of love, light, and genuine service. Having a personal mission statement will quickly get you to align with your commitments.

Your mission statement is based on your commitments. For example:

- I am committed to bringing people together to connect, create, and revive the connection of the human spirit.
- I am committed to loving with my whole heart and listening.
- I am committed to having others feel heard, known, and supported.

My commitments, purpose, and identity are present in my events, my life, my relationships, and my well-being. I get up in the morning, and I go to bed at night with it. My commitment is present throughout this book. No matter what, I live this mission.

This can be as detailed or simple as you like. Most importantly, when you are this clear about whom you help and how you help them, you can put all your energy behind the statement. It must be 100% true for you. If it's true, people will believe it and buy it, but you have to believe it and buy it first.

If you are clear about your commitments, mission, and value, you can bet that you will be able to create any event and fill any room! I am excited to take you into further chapters as we talk about more details in declaring and fulfilling your next event!

ROBYN SCOTT

About Robyn Scott: Robyn is the Chief Relationship Officer for Champion Circle. She manages the prospecting program for Divinely Driven Results. Scott is a Habit Finder Coach and has worked closely with the president, Paul Blanchard, at the Og Mandino Group. She is also a certified Master Your Emotions Coach, through Inscape World. Scott is commonly known in professional communities as the Queen of Connection and Princess of Play. She has been working hard for the past nine years to hone her skills as a mentor and coach.

Scott strives to teach people to annihilate judgements, embrace their own stories, and empower themselves to rediscover who they truly are. Scott is an international speaker and also teaches how to present yourself on stage.

Her first book, *Bringing People Together: Rediscovering the Lost Art of Face-to-Face Connecting, Collaborating, and Creating* was released in August of 2019 and was a bestseller in seven categories.

Author's website: *www.MyChampionCircle.com/Robyn-Scott*
Book Series Website & Author's Bio: *www.The13StepsToRiches.com*

Shannon Whittington

SMALL STEPS INSTEAD OF GIANT LEAPS

I am a dreamer and a risk-taker through and through, but I also know that the road to success is not a straight path. While it's important to dream big and let your imagination run wild, all the dreaming in the world won't amount to much if you don't have a road map to get to your goals. In fact, dreaming without a plan of action can often lead to feeling debilitated and overwhelmed. This is where the brilliance of organized planning comes into play.

Organized planning crystallizes desire into action, where dreams transform into reality. It's the act of taking all of your raw creativity and passion and figuring out what and who you need to make it come to life. While each person's organized plan for success looks different, here are a few tips to help you create your own.

Collaborate!

A lot of us are independently minded, and that's fantastic! But the truth is we don't know everything, and we can't do it alone, even when it comes to making our dreams come true. This is why it's so important to evaluate your areas of strength and weaknesses.

For example, I'm an expert when it comes to LGBTQ+ healthcare. It's my passion, and it drives me every single day. And because so many nurses and clinicians are untrained in this area, I decided to create an online course centered on LGBTQ+ healthcare. I worked on content extensively for months, taking everything I've learned through my certifications and my master's and doctorate programs and turning it into something that healthcare professionals can easily learn and implement into their daily work.

The only problem is that I am far from an expert in I.T., and as I was creating this course, I realized I knew nothing about putting it online. This realization paralyzed me for over a year until I realized that the answer to my problem was right in front of me. I needed to ask somebody for help. In other words, I needed to collaborate!

I have an online connection from LinkedIn, a nurse educator, and also a part of the LGBTQ+ community. We've been friends for a couple of years, and every so often, he would send me a message and say, "We should collaborate." We floated the idea of collaborating for years but never actually made anything happen. I don't know what stopped me, really. Fear of him stealing my idea, maybe? Or maybe taking credit for my work? Who knows? But eventually, I decided to let those thoughts go because I wasn't moving forward. So I reached out to him, and after scheduling a time to chat on Zoom, I not only found out that this man was an I.T. whiz, but he also shared the same goal of creating an online course on the same topic. So we reviewed our outlines for our courses, and they were nearly identical!

Within just a few months, we created a partnership that looks really exciting. We put aside our egos and fears of taking a risk with somebody new, and we turned our shared goal into a reality. Plus, not only do I have a newfound creative and business partner, but a trusted and valued friend as well.

Surround Yourself Accordingly

In the spirit of collaboration, it's vital to surround yourself with people who are just as ambitious and determined as you are. Even if these people have wildly different dreams than you and collaborating on a task may not be a worthwhile endeavor, it is still important to make them your friend, thought partner, coach, or mentor. Who knows what could develop down the line?

If you're a dreamer and ambitious, it can be alienating to be surrounded by people who don't share your level of passion. Ambition, after all, can look extreme to people who have yet to realize their potential. Suppose you find yourself unable to have real or productive conversations about the future, about success, about how to transform your dreams into reality. In that case, it's so easy to let your dreams remain stagnant. However, the possibilities are endless when you immerse yourself in environments where everyone dreams, plans, and makes the most of their talents and passions.

This can be as easy as joining professional networking groups on LinkedIn, Clubhouse, Wisdom, or something similar and making your presence known. By putting yourself out there, sharing your dreams, and bravely opening yourself up to advice, you're introducing yourself to an entire world of inspiration to help you plan your road to success. In addition, taking the seemingly small step out of your comfort zone and surrounding yourself with people talking about how they've achieved success - their endeavors, lessons learned, tips, and tricks - can provide you with more insight than you can imagine.

Be Patient

I've realized that the bigger we dream, the less patient we can be when it comes to achieving our goals. When we work hard, we often fall into the trap of expecting practically overnight results, but that's not the case. Further, when we're so wrapped up in looking at the big picture, it's easy to lose sight of the small steps it takes to succeed. This, too, can lead to abandoning our goals out of impatience, fear of failure, or, frankly, both.

However, the reality is that whatever you want to do, you have to commit to making some form of progress, no matter how seemingly small, every single day. Whether it's reaching out to a potential new colleague or collaborator on LinkedIn, asking a mentor to look over your resume/portfolio, or even engaging in a mindfulness routine to get yourself into a better headspace, each individual step matters. Further, this action can keep you grounded and, at the moment, help you better appreciate the everyday moments that our ambitious and future-focused minds often take for granted.

As a personal example, four years ago, I was asked to speak at a conference about transgender healthcare. My wife and I drove for five hours and covered our entire expenses - transportation, lodging, food, everything - but only ten people were in attendance. Some might consider this a waste of time and resources when I could have been seeking out much bigger opportunities. I certainly thought that at the time. I'm not gonna lie. But because I know how important it is to educate others on this topic, I spoke as if the room was full.

Two years later, I received an email from an attendee at that conference. She mentioned that she was leading a conference about transgender healthcare, and she wanted me to speak. Though she offered an honorarium of $100, I declined the honorarium. Yet again, it was a very small crowd, but I told myself that every presentation I give has the potential to lead to bigger and better things.

This same person recently reached out to tell me that those attendees were still talking about my presentation! So what I deemed a favor in the name of my passion ended up being something that people remembered and discussed years later! Not only that, but this person is also now an event manager for a massive conference focused on gender-related healthcare, and she asked me to speak to an audience of over 1,000 participants! All-expense paid, by the way!

I think about what might have happened, or what might not have happened, had I not driven those five hours to speak to that tiny audience in a dingy hotel conference room. Yet, I remain grateful that I remembered how much each step matters; that if there's even one person in the audience, I should speak as if there are thousands because one day, there very well may be.

Organizational planning isn't always the most fun aspect of achieving your goals. It can be cumbersome to take individual steps instead of giant leaps, force yourself out of your comfort zone and interact with other dreamers, take the risk, and collaborate with others who know things you don't. But I promise that when you commit to making a plan and putting your goals into action, you can and will achieve things you may have never thought possible. So make a plan, make it happen, and watch your reality unfold before your eyes.

SHANNON WHITTINGTON

About Shannon Whittington: Shannon (she/her) is a speaker, author, consultant, and clinical nurse educator. Her area of expertise is LGBTQ+ inclusion in the workplace. Whittington has a passion for transgender health where she educates clinicians in how to care for transgender individuals after undergoing gender-affirming surgeries.

Whittington was honored to receive the Quality and Innovation Award from the Home Care Association of New York for her work with the transgender population. She was recently awarded the Notable LGBTQ+ Leaders & Executives award by Crain's New York Business, as well as the International Association of Professionals Nurse of the Year award. Whittington is a city and state lobbyist for transgender equality.

To date, Whittington has presented virtually and in person at various organizations and conferences across the nation, delivering extremely well-received presentations. Her forthcoming books include *LGBTQ+: ABC's For Grownups* and *Kindergarten for Leaders: 9 Essential Tips For Grownup Success.*

Author's Website: *www.linkedin.com/in/shannonwhittington and on YouTube at ShannonWhittingtonConsulting-for 101 LGBTQ videos*
Book Series Website & Author's Bio: *www.The13StepsToRiches.com*

Soraiya Vasanji

BE WATER

I love making a plan! Seriously! I get excited at the beginning of a new project, idea, or event. I realized that I receive enormous satisfaction from the ideating, constructing, preparing, organizing, completing, and reflecting stages of creating something out of nothing. All of which are the basic building blocks of organized planning. It creates such excitement and joy for me! Organized planning is all about creating and executing systems, where the "organization" component is about the structure, and "planning" can be seen as the sequence of events. As someone who loves to host a party for any and every reason, I strive to make sure everyone has an amazing time from the moment the invitations have been sent out to thanking them for coming. When planning a party, I get satisfaction from the planning stage as much as the actual event! I love figuring out the steps that will be needed to execute or create my desired dream. Then I go about infusing creativity, fun, and celebration along the way! Breaking down a big goal into small achievable steps creates sustainable momentum and helps keep me motivated throughout the process! This is the real game- changer in executing and creating momentum in a project: the carving of big steps into tiny pebbles so they can get accomplished quickly and keep moving.

It is probably why I love 1,000-piece puzzles; I have a systematic approach to these puzzles. Always starting with the edges, grouping colors or parts of images, and then working one by one. It is like a 1,000-piece puzzle is two 500-piece puzzles or ten 100-piece puzzles, or twenty-five 40-piece puzzles. Well, repeating a 40-piece puzzle seems way less daunting than tackling a 1,000-piece puzzle. Am I right? Watching it come together to reveal something that wasn't there before is magical. And why I am now a puzzle collector!

Many people believe breaking things down into steps is important, but it is actually the most important part of creating success. The threat of inaction is too common. The real magic is breaking something down into the tiniest piece that you can't help but complete. For example, in my party analogy, one step may be figuring out the menu. As one step, this may be overwhelming. However, dividing this into a series of steps that includes calling caterers or restaurants for sample menus and pricing is easier. And if this feels overwhelming, then breaking this down into making a list of restaurants to reach out to can be separated. The idea is that if the step is too big, then we get to further divide the step into multiple pieces or stages. There is real magic in breaking down a larger project into simple, easy steps. Otherwise, the feelings of overwhelm creep in!

One of my mentors, Amy Yamada, shared the idea that overwhelm is just in our heads, and either we are not committed or don't have an executable plan, so either we need to get a plan, get committed, or both! I loved this because it highlighted that when I get stuck or start procrastinating, I am unclear on the plan, or the step is too big or not connected to the larger picture. Therefore,

get a manageable plan!
get committed!
get into action!

Viola! It only takes one small step to start inertia and build momentum. How does this work in reality? Think of a large goal or project you have. Now let's break it down. For example, my client wants to build an online course. We start with an outline of her modules, and her first step is to write out module one. It's been a month, and she hasn't started. Do you have a project like this? Where you know your next step, but you haven't jumped into action? When we dug deeper, she was overwhelmed at the idea of everything she had to include in module one. Thus, we broke it down together, and she made a list of all the parts to include. Then she blocked 20–30-minute increments in her calendar and picked 1-3 items to write about. In one week, she wrote all of her content, and because she was so enthralled, she recorded a hysterical, raw, and enticing video demonstrating what she does and who she is. What a difference, right?

How can you break down what has been eluding to you? No step is too small because this is how we build momentum.

In my life, I have always been clear on my 30-year-old plan.

Excellent grades in school-> College -> Undergraduate Degrees-> Find Love & Career -> Job/ Marriage -> Career Success-> Business School->Ideal Job/Career Achievement -> Kids... all by 30!

In each stage of my life, I break down what gets to happen to move on to the next phase. At age 26, I was working a full-time marketing career at Abbvie Pharmaceuticals, going to Northwestern's Kellogg School of Business for my MBA, launching a fast-casual Indian restaurant in downtown Chicago on the side, and my mom was in the hospital in which we later came to learn she has an auto-immune disease called Myasthenia Gravis. Compartmentalizing was one thing but being fully committed to my 30-year-old plan meant I got to be in my A-game, make trade-offs but not let the little things throw me off. Having an organized plan and executing it was what made all the difference.

And you want to know the secret ingredient in this recipe of planning and executing? It all comes down to consistency and believing in your dream. The coolest part is that we get to work on it every day. When it feels too hard, too much, or things don't go as planned, let go. Let go of how you think it has to look. Let go of forcing it. Remember that each day is a brand new day so let it go and get committed again. Life is a series of commitments we make to ourselves. Which commitment are you going to keep to yourself? A plan is only good if you execute it. Keep making a choice. One choice leads to the next choice.

I knew that I wanted to make an impact in my marketing career before having kids, and I had no idea what form that was going to take. When our marketing team had the idea to find a powerful spokesperson to spread awareness of treating hypothyroidism consistently and share their own journey, we partnered with Sophia Vergara. At the time, she was wildly popular for acting in the television show *Modern Family.* She was entertaining a deal with Pepsi, and we knew our small brand could not afford to compete at that level. But our persistence and speaking to her heart made it an easy decision for her to collaborate with us. The Share Your Story campaign was a major success, and upon reflection, this was the mark I yearned to create and empower others to share their story and have a voice, that our condition does not define us, nor are we held back by it.

I now know I was always meant to be an Empowerment Coach. It is not the journey I saw, but I have always held true that I get to share with every person I meet that they matter, their voice counts, and they are the architect of their life. We are never stuck! We always have a choice! And when your vision changes, you get to work with what you have. Get new information and keep reassessing. Keep going, never stop. Can't stop, Won't Stop—so Don't Stop! Life certainly was not how I envisioned it would unfold nor its timing, but when we create a plan, we get to keep working on it. What if at 70% you stop? Who knows, if you kept going, what new decision you would have uncovered at 75% that could have taken you in a whole new direction. So please don't give in to the fear because it's not real. Stay grounded in your vision and keep making progress, no matter how small.

If I had the fear that I would never have a baby, I wouldn't have my beautiful baby girl Naila. And that would have been a real tragedy, for she is the light and love that will truly impact the world. It's important to recognize that plans are "fluid." When things don't work out, it is not necessarily about stopping. It is about shifting. I like to think about water and how it chooses the least resistant path. It is not attached to how it gets there; it just knows it is going in one direction. It is our humanistic tendency to become myopic and fixated on how or what. Instead, be water. Allow your plans to be fluid like water and recognize your thoughts shift on how you get there instead of re-adjusting the goal. My clients trust me to support them in maximizing their best possible chance of having the baby of their dreams, and it may not look like what they thought this part of the journey would look like. And together, we are committed to the ultimate goal and fluid like water.

SORAIYA VASANJI

About Soraiya Vasanji: Soraiya is a Certified Professional Coach (CPC), Energy Leadership Index Master Practitioner (ELI-MP), and has a Master's in Business Administration (MBA) from Kellogg University. She inspires women to be present, not perfect, ditch what doesn't serve them, and create their best messy life now. She loves sharing her wisdom on mindset, the power of language, self-love, self-worth, and leadership principles. She is the founder of the *Mommy Mindset Summit* series, where she interviews experts on topics that interest moms, so they can create a life of authenticity, abundance, and joy—and show their kids how to have it all, too.

Soraiya is married to her soulmate, has a four-year-old daughter, and lives in Toronto, Canada. She is a foodie and a jetsetter, and she loves collecting unique crafting and stationery products!

Author's Website: *www.SoraiyaVasanji.com*
Book Series Website & Author's Bio: *www.The13StepstoRiches.com*

Stacey Ross Cohen

THE ROADMAP TO SUCCESS

"A goal is a dream without a deadline"
- Napoleon Hill, Think and Grow Rich

Napoleon Hill's sixth principle, Organized Planning, is perhaps the most critical part of any business. Creating a roadmap and action plan will help you achieve success.

It's tempting to jump into the tactics like creating a blog or YouTube channel. But you need to be intentional and develop a well-informed strategy to avoid back peddling. Without a clearly defined plan of where you're going and what's needed, your chances of success are slim.

So how do you go about creating this roadmap? By setting goals, taking action, and planning accordingly. This chapter will discuss the importance of each of these steps and how they can help your professional and business growth. Are you ready to map out your success? Let's get started.

Setting the Course

What do successful people have in common, whether a marathon runner, valedictorian, or billionaire? They recognize that goal-setting is essential to their success. Establishing goals provides a sense of purpose and accomplishment once you achieve them.

In our fast-paced world, we often get caught up in day-to-day tasks. Setting goals and putting them into action is vital to success. If you want to achieve anything meaningful, you can't just sit around and hope for it to happen on its own. You need to manufacture your opportunities.

But setting goals isn't as simple as jotting a few sentences down on paper. Goal-setting skills are a real muscle you need to develop — and the SMART approach is a powerful way to drive success.

SMART goals are all that

SMART (Specific, Measurable, Achievable, Relevant, and Time-Bound) is an acronym that you can use to guide your goal setting. It ensures the clarity, focus, and motivation required to craft meaningful goals. Start by envisioning the end-state and reverse engineering it. Let's examine each of these characteristics individually.

Specific. It is essential to be as clear as possible about what you wish to accomplish. An unclear goal will result in wasted efforts (e.g., I want to make more money). Goals should address who, what, when, where, and why. The more narrow a goal, the more you'll be able to detail the steps necessary to achieve it.

Measurable. How are you quantifying your goal? How will you prove you are making headway? Measurable goals allow you to track your progress. Setting milestones along the way will enable you to re-evaluate and course-correct as needed.

Achievable. How realistic is it to attain your goal? First, clear actions or tasks need to be aligned with each goal. Setting goals you can accomplish within a specific time frame will help keep you motivated and focused.

Relevant. Each goal should sync with your values and larger, long-term goals. Explore "the why" behind the goal. Why is this goal important to you? Is working toward this goal worthwhile? How will this help you contribute toward your long-term goals?

Time-bound. What is your goal time frame? A completion date can help provide motivation and help you prioritize. Make sure to assign a deadline to each goal. Planning to fail is a smart move. Consider potential 'what ifs' to develop a more resilient business strategy. Ensuring contingencies are in place if things go wrong will prepare you to survive even the worst-case scenario.

Spring into Action

Identifying your goal is merely the first step. Once it's in your crosshairs, it's time for action.

When I say action, I mean intentional action. Throwing spaghetti on the wall doesn't turn desire into success. Instead, once you've listed 3-5 SMART goals, determine what specific steps are required to reach them and commit to doing whatever is necessary to achieve them.

Next, create a "Must Do" list daily. This is not a typo: "To Do" is too passive, so I prefer to call it a "Must Do" list. Ask yourself: What must I do today to support my purpose and goals? How does this activity support my purpose? Clear goals and Must Do's are critical to transforming goals into reality. As you meet your goals, it's essential to raise the bar.

For me, that happened in 2010 when my passion for marketing and branding businesses morphed into personal branding. At first, this next step in my career was an accident, not conscious goal-setting. I was contacted by an organization that supports the underemployed, unemployed, and career transitioners. "Would you speak to the organization's audience?" the director asked me. I agreed without a specific topic in mind but quickly had an epiphany. This unexpected pro bono speaking engagement helped me realize: Personal brands shouldn't be exclusive to Fortune 500 leaders, celebrities, or powerful politicos. They can and should be tools for everyone, from my daughter in high school to my 75-year-old retired father. Helping people be and communicate their best selves was my new burning desire.

I paired that new desire with goals and a "Must Do" list. And within a few years, I was a contributor on personal branding for the *Huffington Post* and debuted on the TEDx stage.

It's not easy to set goals and figure out what we want in life. Achieving goals requires hard work and commitment. Your ability to follow through and do whatever is necessary is key. A mental game is involved — you have to really want it! Passion, purpose, and a burning desire will help you reach your goals. Keep these seven essentials in mind to achieve your goals:

1. Prioritize your goals: If the goal is truly important to you, treat it as such. Schedule actions related to your goal before other unrelated tasks, and don't procrastinate. Make sure to record your goals in a journal, word document, or app.

2. Commitment: When roadblocks arise to test your resolve, remind yourself why you set the goal in the first place. Revisit your goals worksheet to ensure you stay on track and re-energize. Remind yourself that it will all be worth it in the end.

3. Know yourself and surround yourself with great talent: Self-awareness and understanding your strengths and weaknesses are key. Hire talented people who complement your skill set to take your business to the next level. Also, don't hesitate to seek consultants to bridge any gaps.

4. Create Systems: It's important to have protocols and systems in place to stay on track and reach your goals. With the help of technology tools - from social media to tracking sales – you can streamline processes and manage your business more efficiently.

5. Accountability: Establishing roles and responsibilities and setting deadlines for tasks ensures that each team member knows what is expected of them. This creates an environment of accountability that will scale your business.

6. Make it a habit. You need to stop overthinking and simply DO it! Determine what routine works for you and then put it into practice.

Maintain a constant drumbeat of activity that supports your goals in your everyday life.

7. Maintain flexibility: It's inevitable: You will be thrown a curveball, and the routines and habits you've formed will get messed up. This is where flexibility is critical. Find ways to pursue your goals even as unexpected things happen with relationships, health, or finances.

Remember, plans don't have to be complicated and lengthy, but they must be actionable. A plan that lacks action steps is merely a proclamation.

Measuring Progress

Measure progress against your plan, make adjustments accordingly, and keep pushing forward. Effective planning is an ongoing process, not a one-time event. What does that mean? It means that no matter how well you plan, unanticipated issues will arise, requiring you to modify the plan. In some rare cases, you may need to replace the plan with a new one.

Revisit your plan regularly to ensure that you are on track to achieve your goals. Again, accountability and persistence are key!

Getting to the Finish Line

Maintaining a burning desire to achieve your goals is easier said than done. Obstacles, distractions, and burnout are all common. And so, I'll end with some tips for getting to the finish line. Here are three best practices

1. Feed your mind. Inspirational books and podcasts are a great way to maintain your motivation and drive. My shelves are filled with inspirational business books to build my brain muscle. Here's a sampling: *Mindset: The New Psychology of Success* (Carol S. Dweck, Ph.D.), *Built to Last* (Jim Collins), *Start with Why* (Simon Sinek), and *Thrive* (Arianna Huffington).

2. Surround yourself with positive and successful people. Spend time with family, friends, and business colleagues who "root for you." Alternatively, avoid negative people who sap your energy. As best said by motivational speaker Les Brown: "If you want to fly with eagles, don't swim with the ducks."

3. Make it a habit. You need to stop overthinking and just DO it! In your everyday life, maintain a constant drumbeat of activity. Discover what works for you, and then practice it. You'll be amazed how much energy you have to check items off your "Must Do" list.

You may think that goal setting is all about planning for the future. But in reality, it's also important to take a moment to reflect on your progress. In addition, celebrating accomplishments is a great way to stay motivated and push you to reach and expand your goals. So don't forget to celebrate your wins along the way!

As you seek success, let organized planning be the engine that propels you forward. Identify what you want, figure out how to make it happen, and then get to work. Then, don't stop until that desire is a reality.

STACEY ROSS COHEN

About Stacey Ross Cohen: In the world of branding, few experts possess the savvy and instinct of Stacey. An award-winning brand professional who earned her stripes on Madison Avenue and major television networks before launching her own agency, Stacey specializes in cultivating and amplifying brands.

Stacey is CEO of Co-Communications, a marketing agency headquartered in New York. She coaches businesses and individuals across a range of industries, from real estate to healthcare and education, and expertly positions their narratives in fiercely competitive markets.

A TEDx speaker, Stacey is a sought-after keynote at industry conferences and author in the realm of branding, PR, and marketing. She is a contributor at *Huffington Post* and *Thrive Global,* and has been featured in *Forbes, Entrepreneur, Crain's* and a suite of other media outlets. She holds a B.S. from Syracuse University, MBA from Fordham University and a certificate in Media, Technology and Entertainment from NYU Stern School of Business.

Author's website: *www.StaceyRossCohen.com*
Book Series Website & author's Bio: *www.The13StepsToRiches.com*

Teresa Cundiff

DO YOUR KEYS ALWAYS GO IN THE SAME SPOT?

I begin this chapter with a question because it makes me nostalgic for one of my dearest college sorority sisters. We lost touch after college, which broke my heart, but we are back in touch again, which makes my heart sing. I'll call her Derna Ree because that's something special between us.

Derna Ree would walk into her campus apartment and throw her keys anywhere… just toss them. I don't think she would mind me telling you about her proclivity to throw her keys because it was the cause of much consternation when we would be trying to get out the door of said campus apartment and said keys were nowhere to be found. It was the craziest of all crazy things!

I can remember one time in particular when I thought, "I'm going to keep up with what part of the room she's thrown her keys," but I still wasn't able to track them! It was inexplicable! Now, Derna Ree was super smart, an accounting major, the treasurer of our sorority for two years, if I remember correctly, and graduated to work for one of the Big 4! The chick had brains! But those dang keys! And regardless of whether she lived with a roommate or in a place by herself, we were always on the hunt for her keys!

Now, me? My keys? Always in the same spot… always! I am a creature of habit. I make my bed every day as well, and that was before Admiral McRaven made his now-famous commencement speech and wrote a book about it! I believe that habits and daily routines are the beginnings of Organized Planning which is what we are here to talk about. So, as per my usual, let's examine: Do you consider yourself an organized person?

I'll reveal more about myself to you even though you're reading this to see what's in it for you. Right? I will offer up my thoughts in hopes that you may find application in your life. Please feel free to pick and choose, to accept or reject.

Long ago, I established a centralized place for my husband near where he enters the house to drop his keys and his wallet. This was really a selfish act on my part as I didn't want him always asking me if I had seen his wallet and keys! LOL! It was a small thing but a marriage saver! Again LOL! This location has changed many times since we were an active-duty military family for 20 years, but I always found the place to put his basket shortly after unpacking the kitchen and the wardrobe boxes!

I will confess that my closet floor needs my organizing attention, but that's the one thing I allow myself to slide. I give myself some grace, as it were. And I will also confess that as I type this chapter, my desk needs tidying up. But I function best in an organized world where there is a place for everything, and everything is in its place. I want to be your biggest encourager and cheerleader here to bring your world into order. If you can't do it on your own, find someone to help you, even if you must hire a professional. I'm offering my thoughts and opinions, mind you, so take what you want and leave the rest as I said.

My surroundings must be orderly and organized for me to be at my best for planning because I am a planner! I am a linear thinker! I am a strategic thinker! I am an analyzer! But even with all that in the tank, I still need the help and support of my Mastermind (MM) friends to help me with my plans. Once I've given myself the physical environment for organized planning, I need to further give myself the intellectual environment for organized planning. You see, a truly smart person knows her own limitations and seeks answers and solutions to complement those limitations. Hence, the Mastermind was brought to us by Napoleon Hill. I submit that having a MM group in place is organized planning on your part!

If the plans that I have for my business are on the struggle bus, I can bring them to my MM peeps and talk it out with them. Napoleon Hill says, "You may originate your own plans, either in whole or in part, but see that those plans are checked and approved by the members of your Master Mind alliance." All those good brains are pulling together to support and help you can see things you cannot and can help you adjust your plans! Hill writes, "No man is ever whipped until he quits—in his own mind." And this is what it boils down to.

When the plans I have meet with "failure," that's not precisely what it is. It is merely that the PLAN wasn't sound, not ME! Be sure to separate yourself from the plan! And therein lies the CRUX of it all, right? We think that we and the plan are one! Hill just tells us to adjust the plan and try again! And to keep adjusting until the plan meets with success! And here is where we drag out the ever-popular Edison example of his 10,000 tries to make the incandescent light bulb! But is there a better one? No! Because we all know how the light bulb changed the WORLD! And we draw on Edison as inspiration when we want to quit. Don't quit; just make those adjustments in your plans until you find success! All easier said than done, but that's why having your MM peeps to uplift you and keep you going is super important.

But here is the big question. How long do you keep on keeping on? Right? No one can answer that. Maybe you set a number and say if you aren't turning a profit by this date, you close shop. Or maybe if you haven't attracted X number of clients by this date, you shift your strategy to this. It could be any number of factors, but you set those milestones and put in place your plans to achieve them. Then, when the due date hits, you re-evaluate and make adjustments. It happens every day in life and in business.

When we lived in Ft. Leavenworth, KS, we were blessed to have my cousin and her family live nearby in Liberty, MO. She and I are almost the same age, and our boys are just months apart in age. It was the first time we had ever lived so near family in our whole military career. It was such a fun and exciting time for both of our families! We had more free time, of course, because we had just been dropped there for a year of schooling as my husband attended the Command and General Staff College, but for my cousin, her life was full! She had her horse business; her husband had his pavement sealing business; the boys had their hockey after school.

We would make plans to see each other and call it Plan A. We would talk, and things would still be a go for Plan A. The next thing you know, the phone would ring, and she would say, "We have to go to Plan B." So, Plan B would be formulated, and we would move ahead with that plan. We would not be thwarted however, because it meant that much to us to see each other and for our boys to spend time together. There were times when it seemed like we went to Plan E, but we were flexible that way! We didn't get mad! Neither one of us had failed because Plans A-D hadn't worked! We just kept adjusting until our plans came together, and we were able to finally be at the same place at the same time! We had perseverance and dogged determination for our families to spend time together, and we weren't going to let crazy circumstances get in our way!

My example here may seem like a bit of an oversimplification, but my point remains! First, you must have a plan! You cannot make adjustments to a plan you do not have, nor can your MM peeps help you if you have no plan! Secondly, try not to feel like making adjustments to the plan is a failure on your part. Many things will happen beyond your control. Just incorporate those appropriately, seek counsel if necessary, and keep moving forward if you can. And lastly, I'll revisit this again, find organization in your life. You'll be the better for it!

This chapter from me does require some personal assessment. I didn't even touch on procrastination, but it's just a little tough love, all in the name of helping you, supporting you, and uplifting you! I'm being a MM peep for you! "Winkey Face" Be deliberate, purposeful, and intentional. So I'll begin where I started. Do you know where your keys are?

TERESA CUNDIFF

About Teresa Cundiff: Teresa hosts an interview digital TV show called *Teresa Talks* on Legrity TV. On the show, she interviews authors who are published and unpublished—and that just means those authors haven't put their books on paper yet. The show provides a platform for authors to have a global reach with their message. *Teresa Talks* is produced by Wordy Nerds Media Inc., of which Cundiff is the CEO.

Cundiff is also a freelance proofreader with the tagline, "I know where the commas go!," Teresa makes her clients' work shine with her knowledge of grammar, punctuation, and sentence structure.

Teresa is a two-time International Best-Selling Contributing Author of *1 Habit for Entrepreneurial Success and 1 Habit to Thrive in a Post-COVID World.* She is also a best-selling contributing author of *The Art of Connection; 365 Days of Networking Quotes,* which has been placed in the Library of Congress. She is a four-time best-selling contributing author to *The 13 Steps to Riches* Series.

Author's Website: *www.TeresaTalksTV.com*
Book Series Website & Author's Bio: *www.The13StepsToRiches.com*

Vera Thomas

WRITE THE VISION

And the LORD answered me: "Write the vision; make it plain on tablets, so he may run who reads it. For still the vision awaits its appointed time; it hastens to the end—it will not lie. If it seems slow, wait for it; it will surely come; it will not delay. Habakkuk 2:2-3 (ESV)

Our thoughts become things
Writing them out makes it plain
What we see in our minds can be what we get
What we write is what will be

I believe the referenced scripture pertains to the vision God, the universe, the Holy Spirit, whatever you prefer to call it, gives to us. When the vision is written plainly, it provides clarity. While things may not happen when we want them to, we can have it if we can see it. If we can write it, it can be. Often as Napoleon Hill indicated, "Most of us are "good starters" but poor "finishers" of everything we begin. Moreover, people are prone to give up at the first signs of defeat. There is no substitute for persistence" (Napoleon Hill). To say this does not apply to me at points and times in my life would not be true. We sometimes waste precious time and energy on things not furthering His plan.

Goals are the vision of what we want as individuals, any group or team. As individuals, our vision includes all areas of our life. A few months ago, I revisited my goals and plans. Even though I have taught goal setting, sometimes having another perspective can be helpful. Under the advice and guidance of a coach, I wrote down some audacious goals that I thought were pretty extreme. We are taking action towards all that was written.

I have written out my goals and created vision boards for many years. Sometimes, me included, we get in the way of dreams becoming a reality. Not this time!

In the first book of this series, I talked about the detours, winding roads, and wrong turns that can defer a dream, not the desire. We can let life and these things discourage us to give up. Today, I am here to tell you, write the plan, make it plain, and never, never, never give up.

Writing The Plan

When doing so, think about every area of your life. Follow the guidelines listed below for every area of your life! This may seem a bit much, even tedious, and even time-consuming. However, taking the time for clarity will lead you closer to your passions and vision.

1. Spiritual - Given that we are spiritual beings as well as physical. Goals to enhance one's spiritual connection can include reading, meditation, breathing, and being in nature.

2. Family - How do you see your family? Whether married, desiring to be married, or single. Identifying what you want and expect from relationships can include all aspects of family. One example of a family goal or vision happened just the week after I completed this chapter. We gathered after the unexpected devasting death of my cousin! He was 56 and died suddenly of a heart attack! We all recognized the need to get together on more occasions than funerals. We have children who do not know each other! Granted, COVID prevented in-person connections, however, we could have perhaps been more diligent in making things happen via zoom or

facetime. We have decided to no longer allow "could've, should've, would've, ought to" to have control of our destinies.

3. Career – Whether you are a teenager thinking about your future, a recent college graduate, or a seasoned adult, what does this chapter in your life look like? There is a difference between a job and a career. Whether you are pursuing a career or seeking a job, keep in mind that there is no such thing as staying on a job or in a career on average of 30 years or 40 years. Those times these days are few and far between. I say that to say it is not abnormal to complete a job or career goal every 4 or 5 years. While I have been in my career for 30+ years, I have had many jobs throughout my lifetime. Discover your passion, and you will discover the plan and vision for your career.

4. Education – Education takes on a myriad of forms. Formal college or trade school education, on-the-job training, mentorships, and programs can enhance your educational dreams and vision for yourself. What is your plan for continuing to educate yourself?

5. Creative vision – What artistic vision do you see for yourself? We all have some creative side. It may not look the same as others; it is a gift that is unique to you. Nurture and cultivate with a vision and plan to enhance.

6. Material things or personal satisfaction What are some personal satisfactions? It may include houses, cars, travel, leisure activities, and other things you want in your life.

7. Mental Growth – mindset. What can I do to improve, sustain, and establish a healthy mindset that is positive and affirming? Reading, listening to tapes, or going on platforms like Clubhouse where mental growth occurs 24/7.

8. Emotional – empathy, compassion, kindness, etc. What is my vision/plan to improve my interactions with myself and others? What areas do I need to improve, and what steps do I need to take to make it happen?

9. Financial goals seem to be the one area where a lot of attention is not given early on. I want to encourage financial planning at an early stage. In fact, children should be taught financial literacy from middle school on up. While it is best to set financial goals for your life early on, so many, including me, have not. The point of awareness is the point to start! Ask yourself what are my financial goals and what do I need to do to get there?

10. Commitment to service or social responsibility. We can change the world one person at a time. Ask yourself, what is the vision I see that I can do to make a difference in my life and the lives of others?

This may not be the only chapter in this book to highlight the process for writing the vision/plan using the SMART model for each area indicated above. However, the more you read about it, the more likely you will consider it. Once the plan, goals, and vision are identified and written, determine the steps needed to complete your plans.

1. Specific: be as detailed as you can be. What is it in each area you envision for yourself? Why do you want it? Identify what it looks and feels like.

2. Measurable: How will you know you have accomplished the plan? Be specific in stating the plan. "I will _____ by this time."

3. Attainable: Do you have what it takes to make the vision happen, or can you acquire it? For example, for me to say I will be a scientist is not achievable for several reasons. First, math and science are not my lanes. In high school, I changed my biology class to general science. Dissecting things did not settle well with my stomach.

4. Relevant: How does this goal apply to other areas of my life?

5. Time-bound: Accomplished by what time. There must be a timeline for accomplishing your goals. I can attest that it may not be the exact date; it will be close either before or after that date.

In conclusion, let us recap what we discussed.

Ask yourself why I want this for myself and be as detailed as possible. The sky is the limit. Plans must have a purpose. What is the Why?

Plans need to be as specific as possible. Be specific if you want a house, car, job, or even relationship. What type of car? What color, etc. Where do you want to live? How many bedrooms, baths, etc. What kind of career, job, or business? A business plan will help with clarity.

When planning for a relationship, especially after ending a long-term relationship or marriage, consider taking time for yourself and writing down the type of relationship you want. What is important in your next relationship? Identify must-haves and be clear. Think about family as a whole. If parents, what type of vision do you have for your children. How do other family members impact my family dreams and goals?

I cannot emphasize enough the importance of writing your plans, making them plain, and experiencing the manifestation. Be patient. Things may not happen when we want them to. However, TRUST that they will happen when you are specific and clear, when we use the SMART model to help define our vision and plans for achieving them.

VERA THOMAS

About Vera Thomas: Vera Thomas lives in the state of Georgia. She is to date a 4x best-selling author, podcast host, certified transformation coach and family mediator, Classroom Management Advocate/Trainer/Speaker/poet. She works with parents, children, schools, organizations and churches.

Vera's life story directed her towards work with organizations that provided hope and empowerment to people like her to better themselves. It is her goal to help others overcome a circumstance that diminishes and help them to surge ahead with their dreams. Vera graduated "Cum Laude" with a Bachelor in psychology from Walsh University in Canton, OH.

Vera has worked as a facilitator for more than three decades, which includes developing training programs for youth and adults. Hear her story and think about your own. Vera is available for companies who want to transform their teams or individuals who want to transform their lives.

Author's Website: *www.VeraThomasCoaching.com*
Book Series Website & Author's Bio: *www.The13StepstoRiches.com*

Yuri Choi

JOURNALING YOUR WAY TO CLARITY

When was the last time you sat down and got very clear about what is actually going on in your life? And not just in one aspect, but all the different aspects, such as work or business, finance, spirituality, creativity, relationships, community, health, wealth, mental health, and so on? If someone took a snapshot of your life today, what would that look like? How clear are you of your future visions for three, six, or 12 months from now? What are some specific plans and tools that can help you get there?

As you read these questions above, you might be sitting there wondering, what does this have to do with Organized Planning as this volume suggests for Napoleon Hill principles? Let me explain by telling you something I heard that was really profound regarding why getting clarity is such a powerful part of activating organized planning towards a vision. I was once at a speaker's dinner at the Habitude Warrior Conference after one of the conferences that we would host, and Dan Clark, an international speaker and bestselling author that I get to call a friend and I greatly admire, gave me a big aha moment about what it means to have clarity. He asked the audience, "how many of you have ever ordered an Uber or a Lyft?" Most people raised their hands. "Well, no matter what kind of car is coming to pick you up, with the best intention to take you to your desired destination, it can't take you anywhere unless you clearly know where you are, and you clearly know where you are going."

This resonated with me so deeply because many people say they want to change and want to become better, yet frequently they are not even clear about their starting point in their journey towards their goals. I've found that gaining clarity alone can bring about huge breakthrough moments for a lot of people. Clarity is powerful.

And this is the same thing with any goals we set in life or the transformation journey that we desire to lead ourselves to achieve these goals. Without clarity about where you are and where you are headed, having clarity about what your starting point is, and what your desired vision looks like, you can't plan the route through the action of organized planning.

Only when one is very clear about their starting point and destination can they find, plan, and organize the right vehicles and tools to get them to their final goal. And the Universe cannot conspire for you to create your vision to come to reality.

As a performance coach, I work with many high achievers and entrepreneurs that are burnt out or overwhelmed. In my initial call with my client, which I call a Clarity Call, I go deep into helping my clients uncover what's really going on for them. This is one of the most eye-opening, profound hours that I get to create with my clients because we get to create the clear starting point and the destination, which allows us the space to co-create the roadmap to get there.

And how does clarity inspire change? Let me give you a peek into how I help my clients gain clarity in our initial clarity call and how this leads to change. I once had a brilliant client (we will call him Max for this story) who came to me and was stressed and overwhelmed. He was a high achiever, rockstar soccer player for many years and has achieved great levels of success in many areas of his life and many chapters in his life. However, when he approached me to work with me, he had forgotten his power and authentic confidence that he once used to exude naturally. He wanted to feel like himself again and get back on track as his high-performer self. In the first few minutes of the clarity call, we discovered that one of the disempowering habits he had is to have alcoholic drinks on nights that he was stressed to numb out his feelings instead of committing to a change that would actually create a lifestyle and habits that would create more flow in his life.

To help him get clear on what was actually going on, I went deep into finding clarity around this situation by asking him a lot of questions.

- "How often do you drink alcohol?"
- "How much do you drink on an outing?"
- "How much do you drink per week?"
- "What do you drink?"
- "Why do you drink?"
- "How often are you hungover?"
- "How many hours of productivity do you lose, if any, because you are hungover per week?"

These are some examples of the questions that I asked him. During this call, my client got very clear that he had way more drinks per week than he initially thought he was, and especially when he got clear himself about the "why" he drinks and the cost of his drinking behavior, he decided in that very call that he was going to take a massive break from drinking. This decision alone created a huge breakthrough for him to initiate a bigger shift in his life and business.

Because he was able to do an accurate assessment of himself through this call, he was able to come to his own decision and own the conclusion that he wanted to change, without me ever telling him what to do (as I believe that is never my job to tell my clients what to do).

One of the things I complete with my clients during my High Achiever Club coaching program is also to help them get very clear on what they want to create and cause in three months or six months, or 12 months from this starting point. Getting an accurate assessment of where they are headed is also a very activating factor for my clients in making an empowering shift in their lives for the better.

If you are looking to gain clarity on where you are today and where you are headed, here are a few journaling questions for you.

Health. Wealth. Relationships.

- What's going well for me right now in these areas of my life?
- What are some things I want to change about these areas?
- What are some empowering habits that I currently have that support my growth in these areas of my life?
- What are some disempowering habits or behaviors that I currently have that do not support my growth in these areas of my life?
- What do I want these areas of my life to look like in three months?
- What do I want these areas of my life to look like in six months?
- What do I want these areas of my life to look like in 12 months?
- What tools, training, or habits can I gain or practice to help me get to these goals on time?

Who are the people that can support me in this journey? Who are the experts in my network? Name at least 5-10 in each category. (Challenge: Call, text, or meet in person to share genuine gratitude for these people being in your life. Start a genuine connection from a place of gratitude and abundance).

Getting clear of these through these journaling questions will activate your process of creating an organized plan so that you can get to your goals and visions powerfully. And you deserve to create your visions and desires to come to reality.

YURI CHOI

About Yuri Choi: Yuri is the Founder of Yuri Choi Coaching. Yuri is a performance coach for entrepreneurs and high achievers. She helps them create and stay in a powerful, abundant, unstoppable mindset to achieve their goals by helping them gain clarity and understanding, leverage their emotional states, and create empowering habits and language patterns.

She is a speaker, writer, creator, connector, YouTuber, and the author of *Creating Your Own Happiness.* Yuri is passionate about spreading the messages about meditation, power of intention, and creating a powerful mindset to live a fulfilling life. She is also a Habitude Warrior Conference Speaker and Emcee, and she is also a designated guest coach for *Psych2Go*, the largest online mental health magazine and YouTube channel. Her mission in the world is to inspire people to live leading with L.O.V.E. (which stands for: laughter, oneness, vulnerability, and ease) and to ignite people's souls to live in a world of infinite creative possibilities and abundance.

Author's Website: *www.YuriChoiCoaching.com*
Book Series Website & Author's Bio: *www.The13StepsToRiches.com*

GRAB YOUR COPY OF AN OFFICIAL PUBLICATION
WITH THE ORIGINAL UNEDITED TEXT FROM 1937
BY THE NAPOLEON HILL FOUNDATION!

THE NAPOLEON HILL FOUNDATION
WWW.NAPHILL.ORG

ISBN Paperback: 978-1-637923-21-4

ISBN Hardcover: 978-1-63792-328-3

www.ingramcontent.com/pod-product-compliance
Lightning Source LLC
Chambersburg PA
CBHW051046060526
44539CB00047B/1527